# Law Prompts

**Large Language Models for Lawyers**

JOHN D. GOODHUE

GOODHUE

# DEDICATION

This book is dedicated to all of the individuals, researchers, scientists, and developers who have pioneered advances in artificial intelligence and with respect to large language models.

GOODHUE

# TABLE OF CONTENTS

# FOREWORD

As a former executive director of the Shanghai Office branch of the Jingsh law firm, one of the largest law firms of China, I have witnessed and born responsibility for all aspects of managing lawyers, their technology, and defining and implementing the best processes possible to deliver quality services to clients while also managing rapid law firm growth. Today, I stand at the crossroads of the East and West, dedicating my expertise to bridging the understanding and application of law through my consulting work interfacing between overseas investors and U.S. companies.

I have always understood that the law is not just a profession, it is a service – a service to justice, to society, and to the truth. In that pursuit, every tool, every innovation that can make our work more effective and efficient is invaluable.

It is my honor to introduce "Law Prompts: Large Language Models For Lawyers", a timely work that is set to help lawyers change the way we perceive and employ technology in the legal field. This book provides practical guidance and instruction illuminating the path for practitioners who wish to harness the power of large language models (LLMs) like ChatGPT to enhance their practice.

Throughout my career, I have seen the law evolve – from vast volumes of printed text to digital databases, from isolated practices to interconnected global firms, and now, towards an era where AI models will work alongside lawyers, assisting and enhancing our capabilities. The author of "Law Prompts" has done a remarkable job of sharing his perspectives and useful examples to help readers explore LLMs.

From a law firm management perspective, which is my particular area of expertise, the impact of LLMs cannot be overstated. Efficient operations, time management, and quality service are the cornerstones of a successful law firm. LLMs, as this book illustrates, have the potential to augment all these areas, transforming not just the practice of law, but the management of law firms as well.

The future of law is here, and it is imbued with the power of artificial intelligence. I firmly believe that "Law Prompts: Large Language Models For Lawyers" is an essential read for any legal professional who aspires to stay at the forefront of this exciting evolution in the field. It is an investment in our collective future, a step towards a more efficient, more equitable legal landscape.

In my experience, the mark of a great law firm is not just its ability to win cases, but its commitment to continually learn, grow, and innovate. "Law Prompts" is an embodiment of this spirit of learning and innovation.

Welcome to the future of law. Welcome to the era of large language models.

--Emma Yan

*As an innovative law firm executive and entrepreneur, Emma Yan has managed and rapidly grown law firm offices through acquisitions and expansions. Jingsh Law Firm moved to the Beijing central business district (CBD) in 2014 and went through a period of reorganization where she was a part of a team which developed the firm from a single small office to 44 branches and 355 alliance offices nationwide in China and 5 overseas offices (in Poland, Germany, Toronto, Cambodia, Singapore), as well as 27 international alliance offices. During that period of time, she served as Investment Partner, Executive Director and Director of General Office at the Jingsh Headquarters in Beijing, Executive Director of Jingsh Zibo in Shandong Province, and Founding Partner, Executive Director, and Director of the Practice Disciplinary Committee of Jingsh International Headquarters in Shanghai.*

*In the U.S. she has founded World Legal Resources based in Washington, D.C. to help attorneys network across cultures. She has also founded AMCW Investment based in Maryland. She consults for investors, seeking value-based investment opportunities.*

GOODHUE

# Law Prompts

## Large Language Models for Lawyers

JOHN D. GOODHUE

GOODHUE

# PREFACE

Halfway through a career as a lawyer, I still marvel at how technology has fundamentally changed the daily tasks of a lawyer. Almost 25 years ago, client communications involved sending and receiving mail once a day and sending an occasional urgent fax. Legal research was performed in a library with books. Paper filing anything was a long and involved process, and often unforgiving. If you ever had to mail something after hours without the help of staff, you know. If you are a young lawyer, you likely cannot even fathom the brutally archaic ways of the 20th Century your more seasoned colleagues endured. Yet, despite all of these changes of the last 25 years, we are in the midst of a transformation which will be even more significant and will occur much more quickly. You do not want to blink and miss it only to find that your methods of practice are outdated, and you are irrelevant.

The tools to analyze information, and generate information are revolutionizing the practice of law and changing the landscape quickly. As a patent attorney with a computer engineering education, and experience as a software developer, those experiences equip me well to see and understand technologies. Never have I seen a shift as significant as we are witnessing today.

A substantial portion of this is the innovation of the large language model (LLM). This is the technology behind innovations such as OpenAI's ChatGPT. The purpose of this book is to introduce large language models in a way to help understand the significance they have in the practice of law amongst many other applications and how they will change your life. Then, to provide some examples of how they can be used to support your practice which involves understanding limitations of both particular LLMs and yourself, and thoughts on improving your ability to "prompt engineer" or "prompt lawyer", which relates to honing your skill in asking the right questions in the right way to obtain the information you want.

Numerous examples of prompts and outputs are included throughout. In some instances parts of the prompts or the outputs are omitted. In other instances, complete outputs are shown. The decisions as to what to show and what not to show were very deliberate so as to avoid unnecessary duplication, to make sure more interesting outputs were included, or to demonstrate specific teaching points.

As a patent and intellectual property lawyer, many of the examples focus more on what I know and what I use, so my apologies to those who find the area of practice uninteresting. However, most prompts can readily be adapted to other areas of law or practice.

One way to use this book is to peruse the examples, finding the prompts which are interesting to you, and ideally trying them for yourself and modifying them to meet your needs. The prompts and outputs should be easy for you to identify as the following convention is normally used.

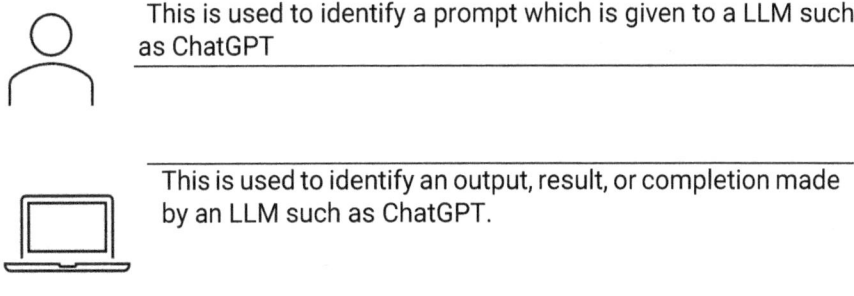

This is used to identify a prompt which is given to a LLM such as ChatGPT

This is used to identify an output, result, or completion made by an LLM such as ChatGPT.

In some instances output is provided in the form of a screenshot or other format.

Most of the examples were performed using OpenAI's ChatGPT using GPT4. Some examples include web browsing functionality. There are a few instances of Google Bard and Microsoft Bing (which incorporates GPT4) throughout, but they are identified as such.

GOODHUE

CHAPTER ONE

# Introduction to large language models for lawyers

Large language models are a truly remarkable technological advancement that has been gaining popularity in recent years. These computer programs are designed to mimic human language and are capable of generating highly realistic and natural sounding text. They are algorithmic in nature and are trained on vast amounts of written and spoken text, making them incredibly versatile and capable of managing a variety of tasks requiring language processing.

One of the most impressive features of large language models is their ability to produce highly sophisticated output that is nearly indistinguishable from human-generated text. They can be used to generate anything from short snippets of text to entire novels, and can be tailored to specific genres or writing styles. In addition, large language models are highly adaptable, with the capability of learning and adjusting based on user interactions.

Early language models were limited in size and complexity. They consisted of small, manually created databases that contained vocabulary and grammar rules. These databases were used to generate text, often in the form of chatbots, that could respond to simple prompts or questions. Sometimes, even correctly! While these early language models showcased the potential of natural language processing, they were often riddled with errors and lacked the fluidity of human conversation.

The size and complexity of language models have grown enormously over time, largely due to advancements in machine learning techniques. Instead of manually creating databases, modern language models use enormous amounts of data to learn patterns and structure in language. This data is often obtained from sources such as books, websites, and social media.

Have you had a close and long-term relationship with a friend, co-worker, or family member where you could finish their sentences? After years of interacting with them, you knew what they were going to say next, or at least an approximation of it? That is analogous to a language model, which instead of being trained with years of personal interactions, is trained with a large set of data and ability to predict what is said next.

Sophisticated examples of these language models, such as GPT-4, boast billions of parameters and are capable of generating highly sophisticated and coherent text. These models are trained on massive amounts of data and use complex algorithms to analyze patterns and structures in language. They have the ability to parse complex sentences and can even generate original content that is indistinguishable from that written by a human.

From small, manually created databases to massive models capable of generating highly sophisticated text, the advancements in natural language processing have brought about a revolution in the way we interact with machines. The scary thing is that this evolution is far from complete.

### *Key Components of Large Language Models*

Large language models are a revolutionary tool for lawyers, offering unprecedented language processing capabilities that promise to advance the delivery of legal services. These models are based on a complex mathematical algorithm that allows them to analyze vast amounts of text data, offering insights that were previously impossible to obtain.

At their core, large language models are essentially advanced statistical models that are trained on large data sets. They use a technique called natural language processing (NLP) to analyze text data and recognize patterns in language usage. This allows them to effectively "learn" language by identifying common linguistic structures and syntax.

In practice, large language models can be used for a wide range of legal tasks. For example, they can be used to analyze contracts, identify key features, and flag any potential issues or red flags. They can also be used to predict the outcome of legal cases, identify trends in case law, and even draft legal documents.

Perhaps most impressively, large language models are capable of generating new text that is grammatically correct, stylistically appropriate, and semantically meaningful.

Overall, large language models represent a major breakthrough in the field of NLP and offer significant potential for lawyers and legal professionals. Whether you are looking to analyze legal documents, predict legal outcomes, or draft legal documents, or manage the business of your law practice, large language models offer an incredibly powerful tool that can save time, increase efficiency, and boost your overall effectiveness as a legal professional.

## *OpenAI and ChatGPT*

OpenAI's introduction of ChatGPT brought large language models into mass consciousness. ChatGPT's ability to generate more accurate and contextually relevant responses, its enormous data set, and its intuitive user interface allowed for immediate adoption.

One of the obstacles to applying AI to a particular problem is the training required. Massive amounts of quality data points may be needed, depending upon the particular problem. This can involve a huge cost to obtain the data as well as to process it. To reduce the training resources required, one could simplify the problem and many different AI implementations have developed to address specific problems.

The language model behind ChatGPT uses a Generative Pre-trained Transformer (GPT) trained for natural language processing tasks, including text generation, using a massive amount of training data diverse in nature. This allows some tasks to be performed with zero-shot learning.

Zero-shot learning is a machine learning approach where a model can generalize to new tasks without having been explicitly trained on them. The result is that ChatGPT provides a very accessible large language model which can be used on many diverse types of tasks without additional training or fine-tuning. The only input needed is the user supplied prompt which is generally in the form of a question or instruction. Thus, engineering the appropriate prompt is of critical importance in order to obtain the desired results.

When using ChatGPT, the prompt provides the user input, the training provides additional input, and then the output is generated. Sometimes the output is called completion. In the context of a GPT model, the process involves understanding the given context of the prompt and predicting the most likely sequence of words to follow in order to provide a coherent and relevant response. Thus, the output is in response to the prompt is text generated to complete the provided input.

OpenAI has a number of different large language models. There is a GPT-4 set of models, a set of GPT-3.5 models, a set of GPT-3 models all of which can be used for natural language. OpenAI has other models too, including Whisper for converting audio into text, and DALL-E for generating and editing images based on a natural language text. Here, we focus on using text applications and not generating images.

## *OpenAI API*

OpenAI provides an application programming interface (API) which is available to developers so that the functionality of its models may be incorporated into their applications. So for example, an input from a web application of a third party may submit a query to OpenAI's servers and receive a response containing a completion. OpenAI charges a small fee for each use with pricing based on the model being used and the number of tokens used. The number of tokens used relates to the size of the prompt and response in the context of natural language queries.

Many of the different AI applications which have hit the market in recent months are using OpenAI's API. These AI applications may add value by using fine-tuned models to provide better context for a particular use case, specific prompts or prompt chains, or other integrations.

## GPT-4 and Microsoft Bing

Microsoft has incorporated a variant of GPT-4 into its Microsoft Bing search engine. It adds to the functionality of ChatGPT in that related search results are provided as well as sources for information. For some uses, including performing research, this can be exceptionally useful.

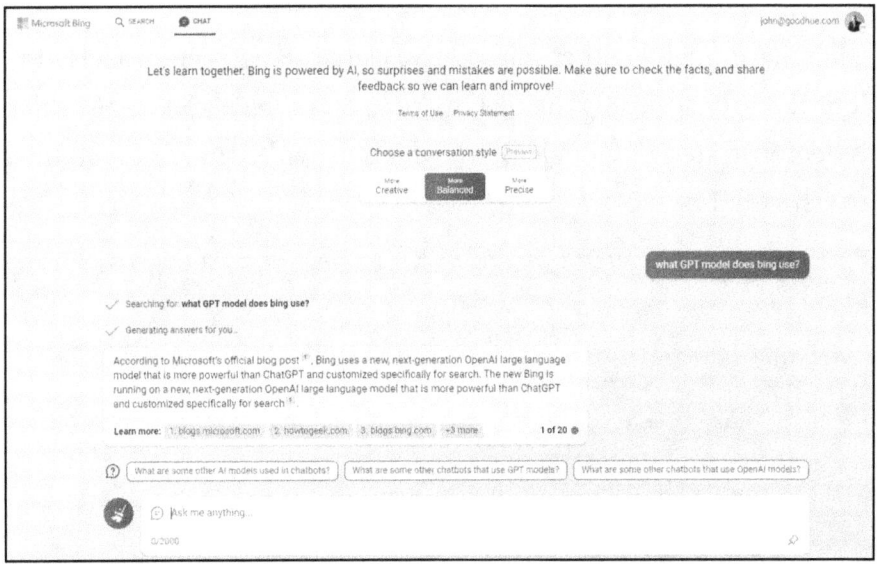

*Screenshot of Microsoft Bing. Copyright Microsoft Corporation*

Microsoft's relationship with OpenAI in addition to ChatGPT's large user base makes it more reasonable to conclude that efforts spent understanding how to generate better prompts in ChatGPT will result in knowledge learned being useful in the future as well as the present. In addition, due to the use of OpenAI's API by a number of different developers, learning to create better prompts in

ChatGPT will likely help in understanding and using some of these special purpose applications.

Some case management and other legal tools are already integrating OpenAI's API or have announced plans too. So experience with ChatGPT should be transferable to future products.

### *Alternatives*

There are many other alternative large language models and interfaces for accessing them. This includes Google's LaMDA which is demonstrated in Google Bard, which provides similar capabilities to ChatGPT.

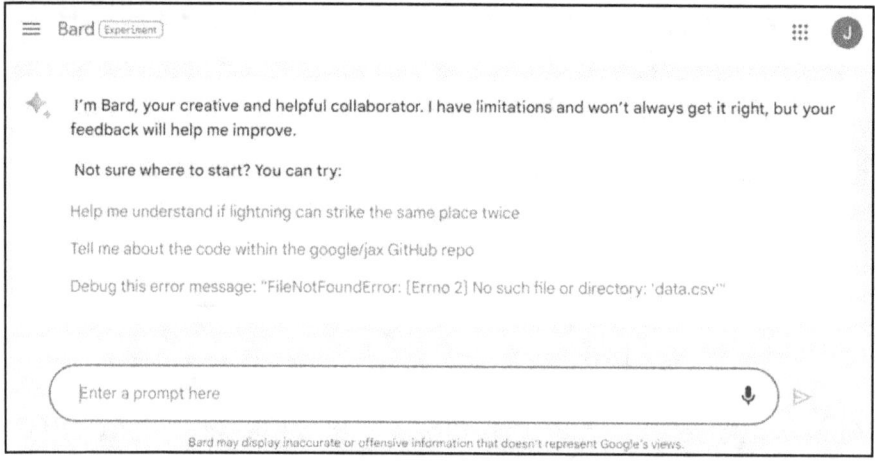

*Screenshot of Google Bard. Copyright Google, LLC.*

Yet there are many other alternatives large language models including Hugging Face's BLOOM, Meta's Llama, Databrick's Dolly and many more. There are conversational AI interfaces available to these large language models.

There are also large models which you may install locally, albeit with smaller training sets. Some of these are open source. Examples include Vicuna, Alpaca, GPT-J, and no doubt there will be many more.

### *Future Growth and Considerations*

The future will include LLMs trained on greater amounts of data, LLMs trained on particular data sets such as legal specific training, tools to better train the large language models or fine tune large language models with your own data using tools such as LangChain. Access to LLMs will continue to be integrated into software products and web sites as a matter of course.

Some models are proprietary like those available from OpenAI, there are other models which are open source such as Dolly 2.0 from Hugging Face. So expect increasing numbers of models all evolving quickly and expanding functionality as they do.

# CHAPTER TWO

# Ethical considerations for lawyers using language models

Whenever we use new technology as lawyers, we need to identify how our use of the technology might affect our ethical obligations so we can adapt our use in ways consistent with those obligations. Therefore we provide a brief discussion of some of the most significant issues.

## *ABA Model Rules of Professional Conduct and Language Models*

When evaluating the impact of technology on attorney ethical obligations, two significant concerns are always competence related to use of technology and confidentiality.

### *Competence and the Use of Technology*

The American Bar Association (ABA) Model Rules of Professional Conduct provide guidelines for the ethical practice of law. In particular, Rule 1.1 states that lawyers must provide competent representation to their clients. This includes the knowledge, skill, and preparation reasonably necessary for the representation.

With advances in technology, lawyers have new tools at their disposal that can aid in their representation of clients. However, to utilize these tools effectively, lawyers must understand how to use them competently.

The ABA Comment to Rule 1.1 specifically addresses the use of technology in the practice of law. The comment states that lawyers should keep abreast of the benefits and risks associated with technology in order to provide competent representation to their clients.

Certainly, Large Language Models including OpenAI's ChatGPT are a technological advancement which can be extremely useful for lawyers in a variety of contexts and situations. Benefits can include significant reductions in time to perform a task and if used appropriately, improved quality in work product. However, there are a number of potential risks.

As previously mentioned, large language models are trained on vast amounts of text data in order to generate responses to a given prompt. However, not all the training data is accurate. Perhaps, there were factual errors in the training, perhaps the information was supposed to be a parody or satire and not factual and this context was not recognized. Perhaps the training data was correct at the time but is now outdated.

In addition to the training itself, the algorithms involved may not accurately identify the context resulting in additional potential for errors.

Thus, competent use of Large Language Models likely requires recognition that factual errors may occur and then either taking actions to mitigate the occurrence of errors and/or to recognize or check for errors in outputs. Although this will be discussed in more detail later, tools like ChatGPT will create citations to cases, articles, and studies that do not actually exist and misunderstand those that do. So one cannot and should not rely on LLM for case law research without checking the sources. This might involve the manner in which prompts are formulated, mental processes to check the accuracy, or additional interaction with AIs or reference sources to verify.

## *Confidentiality and Data Privacy Concerns*

Confidentiality and data privacy concerns have become increasingly relevant in today's digital age, particularly in the legal profession. It is essential to safeguard client information, and lawyers have the legal responsibility to ensure that their clients' data is kept confidential.

 What are some useful questions to ask when evaluating the confidentiality of a large language model service?

> ➤ Data storage and retention: How long does the service store user data and queries? Is the data encrypted at rest and in transit? What are the data deletion policies?

> ➤ Access control: Who has access to the user data and generated outputs? Are there strict access control policies and mechanisms in place to prevent unauthorized access?

> ➤ Data usage: Is the user data used to improve the model or for any other purposes? Are there any opt-out mechanisms to restrict the use of user data for training or other applications?

> ➤ Anonymization: Are there any anonymization or pseudonymization techniques applied to user data to protect the user's privacy and identity?

➢ Compliance: Does the service comply with data protection regulations and standards, such as GDPR, CCPA, or HIPAA?

➢ Security measures: What security measures are in place to protect user data from breaches, leaks, or unauthorized access? Are there regular security audits, vulnerability assessments, and penetration testing conducted?

➢ Third-party sharing: Is user data shared with third parties? If so, under what conditions and for what purposes? Are the third parties bound by the same confidentiality and data protection standards?

➢ Incident response: Is there an incident response plan in place to address potential data breaches or security incidents? Are there clear procedures for notifying users in case of an incident?

➢ Transparency: Does the service provider offer clear and transparent information regarding their data protection practices, privacy policies, and terms of service?

➢ Data sovereignty: Where is the user data stored and processed? Are there any implications related to data sovereignty and compliance with local regulations?

The list above was generated by ChatGPT (Model GPT-4) in response to the prompt above.

Generally, these types of questions can be addressed through examination of Terms of Service and Privacy Policies. Of course, the same company may have different policies for different products. For example, OpenAI has different policies related to its API services than for its ChatGPT service. Thus, to maintain greater confidentiality, lawyers may not want to use ChatGPT but to use applications which use the OpenAI services. This is addressed in section 3(c) of OpenAI's terms of use which are reproduced below.

> *(c) Use of Content to Improve Services. We do not use Content that you provide to or receive from our API ("API Content") to develop or improve our Services. We may use Content from Services other than our API ("Non-API Content") to help develop and improve our Services. You can read more here about how Non-API Content may be used to improve model performance. If you do not want your Non-API Content used to improve Services, you can opt out by filling out this form. Please note that in some cases this may limit the ability of our Services to better address your specific use case.*

Data privacy and large language models has been an area of international concern and going forward we may see more restrictions on use of data, and more comprehensive options to better protect data due to regulatory pressures and market demands. One of the issues has been whether the LLM service provider can use the customer's data in order to improve its model or not. At the time of writing, OpenAI's policies for ChatGPT allow a user to opt-out of having its content used for training while OpenAI's API services by default do not use user content for training. So when API services are used instead of ChatGPT, greater privacy is maintained.

Overall, confidential and data privacy concerns are not so different than any other cloud-based services including internet search engines with the exception of whether data is used to train its models. As a general rule, if uncertain, do not include confidential information or information which can be used to identify a client.

## *Bias*

The American Bar Association (ABA) Model Rules of Professional Conduct provide guidelines for legal professionals to maintain ethical standards in their practice. While these rules do not specifically mention artificial intelligence or language models like ChatGPT, they do contain provisions that are relevant to the issue of bias.

> *Rule 8.4 (Misconduct) is particularly applicable to addressing bias. It states that it is professional misconduct for a lawyer to:*

> *"(d) engage in conduct that is prejudicial to the administration of justice;*

> *...*

> *(g) knowingly manifest bias or prejudice based upon race, sex, religion, national origin, disability, age,*

> *sexual orientation, or socioeconomic status in the course*
> *of representing a client; or*
>
> *(h) engage in any other conduct that adversely*
> *reflects on the lawyer's fitness to practice law."*

Using large language models in the practice of law raises concerns about potential biases that may inadvertently be present in the model's training data. These biases could affect the quality of legal advice provided by the model, and if not addressed, could lead to conduct that might be considered prejudicial to the administration of justice or manifestation of bias as outlined in Rule 8.4.

To mitigate potential bias when using large language models like, legal professionals should:

> ➢ Be aware of the limitations and potential biases in the technology.
>
> ➢ Monitor and assess the AI-generated advice or information for potential biases before relying on or sharing it with clients.

By being vigilant and taking these steps, legal professionals can work to uphold the ethical standards set by the ABA Model Rules of Professional Conduct while leveraging the benefits of large language models in their practice.

In addition to the ethical issues under the Model Rules an attorney may have with using AI tools, there are a host of other potential legal issues or other ethical issues which could affect how an attorney chooses to use tools. Are there data privacy and security concerns beyond or separate from ethical obligations? Must one provide attribution to the LLM used to generate content? How does one best provide attribution when using an AI model? Who owns the output? Does the owner of information used in the training data have any rights in the data which may give rise to copyright infringement or other claims? Is use of an LLM to generate content considered plagiarism? Are some uses of LLM to generate content considered plagiarism? As with any new technology issues will abound and although fascinating to discuss are outside the scope of this publication. However, a starting point for addressing some of these issues is the terms of use of the particular LLM being used.

GOODHUE

# CHAPTER THREE

# Limitations of large language models and their users

Specific implementations of Large Language Models do have their own individual limitations. Generally, these limitations relate to the training of the Large Language Model, constraints in its use. These are not necessarily limitations regarding the capabilities of how it can be used. Users of LLMs also have their own constraints, some of which can be overcome, one of these is difficulty in in remembering that an LLM is not human.

## *Basic limitations of LLMs*

Some of the limitations related to understanding and knowledge, confabulation or hallucination, and lack of real-time knowledge.

### *Understanding and knowledge*

LLMs generate text that may seem knowledgeable and insightful, but they do not understand the text as a human would. The text generated is simply based on patterns. One way to think about this is that an LLM mimics human expressions of understanding and knowledge. Doing so does not actually require any actual understanding or knowledge by the machine.

## *Confabulation or hallucination*

Confabulation is when an LLM generates information that may seem plausible but is fictional. This may be because some training data was fictional. This is particularly important to be aware of. For example, ChatGPT has been known to create fictional legal precedent, fictional scientific studies, and fictional events. It even now includes the warning that "ChatGPT may produce inaccurate information about people, places, or facts". This is, of course, an absolutely critical issue.

### *Real-time knowledge*

LLMs are trained on static datasets and so there is a cutoff date to a LLM's training data. Some LLM implementations are able to supplement this with browsing data and so may be able to identify current information, but the cutoff date for training is still an important limitation.

### Size and contents of training data

In addition, to the cutoff date for its training, the size and contents of the data set will limit the performance of an LLM. Different LLMs and different versions of LLM's will have different training sets. The larger a data set is, likely the more diverse and comprehensive the data which the model is exposed to during training. Sometimes the size of the training set is used to provide one measure of how comprehensive the training set is. For example, the GPT-3 large language model was trained with 45 TB of text data.

Another measure of the training data is the number of parameters. The number of parameters characterizes the size or complexity of training. GPT-3 was trained with 175 billion parameters while GPT-4 is estimated to be trained with 100 trillion parameters.

It is also important to recognize that the size of the training set and the number of parameters does not necessarily indicate better results. This may mean more exposure to biased, inaccurate, or otherwise inaccurate training data which will result in undesired results. Ultimately, different models and different training sets may be better suited to performing particular tasks regardless of the size and contents of the training data.

## *Context window size*

An often critical limitation associated with LLMs such as GPT 3 and GPT4 is the context window. The "context window" refers to the amount of recent conversational window that the model can take into account when generating a response. So this includes both the prompts you input as well as the responses. When the content of a conversation exceeds the size of the window then earlier parts of the conversation are forgotten

Thus, if you are engaged in a lengthy conversation with ChatGPT, the earlier parts of the conversation will eventually be lost, and so subsequent responses may not be informed by that earlier context. To complicate this somewhat, you do not receive any notification of when this occurs.

If you provide detailed context, you may find that due to the context window limitations the model may not be able to generate a meaningful response or as detailed a response as you require. Similarly, certain tasks which require a large amount of information at once, such as reading, summarizing, or editing a long document can be difficult or impossible if the information exceeds the model's context window.

This can limit the usefulness of a LLM significantly if you are working with long documents or sets of documents which might require a significant amount of context. If you include more information as a part of the prompt, then fits within the context window then your input may be truncated and not considered at all. Although you could, of course, break a document in smaller pieces, you will lose context by doing so and will not be as likely to get the results that you want.

To add a further wrinkle to understanding context window size, the context window size is not specified in terms of words or characters, but rather by tokens. A single token might equate to a single character, and it might equate to a word, so if, for example, you are using ChatGPT, you will not know how many tokens are used in your input or your output.

The OpenAI API, used by developers, allows for calculating the number of tokens of a prompt and specifying how many tokens to be used in the response. The OpenAI API's pricing is based on token usage.

## *Not a person*

Inevitably, it becomes difficult if not impossible not to personify ChatGPT or other AI tools. Indeed, presenting information in a chat format or speaking with an AI assistant provides user interfaces which are familiar to us. Many AI assistants even have human sounding names! So it is only natural to treat AU as a person.

Yet when we personify an AI assistant or system, we should remain cognizant that it is not a person. We should also consider how our personification of the AI may constrain our ability to effectively use it as a tool. Too often our interactions with an AI are limited or inefficient not necessarily because of limitations of the AI, but because of our own limitations in our interactions.

## Social overhead

Often, as demonstrated in some of the examples throughout, I impose social overhead into my communications with ChatGPT. I may preface my instruction with a "Please" or include other niceties or social conventions. Although, this may be a best practice for working with a human assistant, it does not improve the interaction with ChatGPT and is an unnecessary inefficiency for both me and for ChatGPT.

If you find yourself including this type of social overhead to your prompts it may be an indication that you are forgetting it is not human. This is certainly not a horrible error to make, but an opportunity to remind yourself that it is not a person and so neither emotional intelligence nor interpersonal skills are required!

## Form of the question

When we ask a person to answer a question or to perform a task and they do not know, generally we believe they understood the context and intent of the question. If an LLM does not give you the answer you are looking for, often the response is really just an objection to the form of the question. So try reformulating the question and asking again. Perhaps providing additional context or otherwise reducing ambiguity will generate better results.

## *Task Decomposition*

When instructing others to perform work, we often decompose a task into a series of sub-tasks either to make the process easier to follow or so that we can check their work and make corrections along the way. If a struggling law clerk is doing the work, we may be more likely to manage in that way. For the rising star associate, we likely expect them to just know what we want and perhaps instruct them to "Please handle" and reasonably expect that is all that is needed to in order to receive work product in good form for review.

When using LLMs, task decomposition is extremely useful to obtain desired results when we can identify a number of explicit steps. However, oftentimes we can combine all of these steps into a single prompt in order to get desired output, we do not need to ask in separate prompts and check the work after each prompt. So it may be a bit like a struggling law clerk and a rising star associate at the same time.

## *Speed*

Of course, the huge benefit that LLMs can provide over humans is speed. Output is generated more quickly and so is available for immediate evaluation. There is no question of when a task is to be performed or how long it will take, it will start immediately, and output will be immediately. Therefore, if your instructions were apparently unclear or ambiguous, you can provide them again.

33

## *Iterations*

A closely related concept is the use of iterations to get the output you need. Because of the speed, you have time to make multiple iterations. When dealing with a person, you might be conditioned to return an assignment to the person once or maybe twice before you make do with what they provide and spend your time revising it. When working with an LLM, you do not have the delay between when you return the work and when you see it again. You do not have to worry about the LLM's perception of the situation where you have asked them to redo the same project five times because they did not do as you intended. So, if you do not receive the results, you are looking for, try different iterations, until you get what you want. Often times, more detailed instructions, examples, or other context will improve the results.

## *Not just source code*

One can also misunderstand LLMs if one thinks of them as traditional computer programs like perhaps one studied in high school or college. When one thinks of LLMs this way they tend to envision a very defined and precise logical operation where when executed the source code will receive input and produce output according to a particular set of program instructions. There are some important distinctions.

LLMs are data-driven, relying on large data sets to learn and generate text. So performance is based on the quality and quantity of the training data. This is different than conventional computer programs which do not require training data and instead have their functionality determined by programmers who explicitly program rules, algorithms, and instructions.

One of the natural consequences of these differences is that LLMs are often considered "black boxes" because even for experts it is challenging to determine how a specific output was arrived at given the complexity of the model and the massive number of parameters involved. Moreover, due to the statistical nature of the LLMs, the same inputs will likely result in different outputs or at least different expressions of the same output.

# GOODHUE

# CHAPTER FOUR

## General guidance on prompts

For general purpose LLMs which have not been specifically trained for specific purposes, one is not going to rely on them for legal advice as they may not be accurate and reliable, may not be able to tailor information for a particular jurisdiction or for individual circumstances. That does, however, mean that they are not incredibly useful tools.

## *Context*

The prompt is how you program the LLM to produce the output you desire. Constructing an appropriate prompt to use with an LLM is a different skill set than formulating an internet search or a case law search. It is also a different skill than cross-examining a witness or drafting an interrogatory. Yet, formulating questions or instructions to get the answers you want will draw upon these other life experiences you may have.

Here, one of the primary concerns when formulating a prompt is to provide sufficient context. An LLM will interpret your request in order to determine a context. The more context you provide, the more specific the context, the greater the likelihood the LLM will get it right.

How do you communicate context? Being clear about what you want, why you want it, how you are going to use it, will all help provide context. Consider if there is any ambiguity in your prompt and remove the ambiguities.

 What are 20 common actions which LLMs can perform and which they are generally considered to be good at??

Perhaps I am interested in large language models, but without sufficient context there is ambiguity in my prompt and thus I should not be surprised to receive an answer such as this:

 LLMs, or Master of Laws degree holders, are often experienced in legal research and analysis, and their advanced training allows them to specialize in specific areas of law. Here are 20 common actions that LLMs can perform:

Often times, providing examples will help provide context in order to show what you want. Sometimes, providing context may involve cutting and pasting information or providing some other input which is to be acted upon or otherwise used in order to generate the output.

## Classifying your use

Sometimes it can be helpful to classify your particular use of an LLM.

### Know v. do not know

Often times we may be asking for it to generate content, compile information, or otherwise product results which we can readily confirm as accurate or inaccurate based on our knowledge and experience. In these types of situations we are the experts, and we are using the LLM tool to help express our thoughts or generate routine output more quickly than we can do ourselves. This type of use is a wonderful use of LLMs to save you time. We "know" what we are looking for and "know" that if the results are accurate or not.

Other times we may ask for specific information not actually knowing what the answer is, this is where using an LLM can be problematic if we assume the answer generated is correct or even if it is a good answer. We simply do not know for certain. There may be steps we can take to reduce the likelihood of obtaining information, which is not correct, but we are not in a position to evaluate.

Classifying how you are using ChatGPT in this way can be useful in how you construct your prompts and how you evaluate the results. If you do not know what kind of output you want generated than more general, open-ended prompts may be used. Often these types of prompts are formulated as questions. Certainly, this is a useful way to learn something.

If you precisely know the type of output you want, then you should write a detailed prompt in order to obtain exactly what you want. Many of the examples throughout this book are in the form of detailed and specific prompts to illustrate the power in providing the proper input to receive the output you want.

When you know what you want, it is easy to evaluate whether the LLM performed the task that you wanted. However, if you do not know something, you are at a disadvantage when it comes to evaluating the accuracy of the results. So, it is especially important to verify the accuracy, relevance, and completeness of the results.

This does not apply only to legal research but to every area of inquiry. If we are prompting an LLM to write search engine optimized content for a web site, it will do so. But how do we know that it did what was asked? If the information presented is outside of our knowledge and experience, we are at a disadvantage.

What makes this type of output even more difficult to evaluate is that, even if it is completely wrong, it may superficially appear correct. If you were to ask a law clerk to research a topic and provide an answer to a question you did not know the answer to, you might question the accuracy of the answer more based on other easier to evaluate indicators of quality such as grammar, spelling, awkward phrases, poor logic, etc. as well as past experience. You may not have any of those type of indicators in LLM-generated content. Instead, you may receive beautifully written prose which flows naturally, and has other hallmarks of quality information consistent with your prior experience, yet the content you receive may be absolutely wrong. Therefore, if you plan to use the results from an LLM you should give some thought as to how you can verify the accuracy of the information presented.

## Facts v. ideas

Another way to classify your use is whether you are looking for facts or ideas. Facts are specific information which may be correct or incorrect. Ideas are possibilities for you to consider. If you want ideas, then more open-ended prompts are helpful. If you are asking for facts, then confirming the accuracy of the facts becomes more important. If you are merely asking for ideas, then you understand it is up to you to decide whether it is a promising idea or not.

## *Front and back matter*

In ChatGPT and many other LLM models, the response is often prefaced with information such as qualifications, statements regarding the limitations of AI, or a re-statement of what it was asked to do, or a reminder that this is an AI system. After the response, additional explanatory information or qualifiers may also be included. Sometimes this information may be helpful. Other times it may not be and so one can suppress it by clarifying in the prompt that it should be suppressed.

Once you have developed your own prompts or become familiar with particular prompts, you likely do not want or need this extraneous information. It may save you time if cutting and pasting results into other documents. In other situations, where there are concerns with running into context window limitations, it will save some tokens.

## *Hallucination avoidance*

In LLM, sometimes incorrect information is provided which is sometimes referred to as hallucination as previously explained. This may involve making up a case citation, a name, an event, or something else.

Sometimes it is as if the LLM is so eager to please you it will provide you with the answer it thinks you want, even if it is wrong.

Sometimes, one can reduce the likelihood of this by including within the prompt that results be verified or checked.

Provide only accurate information which has been verified

Does including language like the above in your prompt mean that only accurate and verified information will be provided? No, but including language like this within a prompt appears to increase the likelihood that accurate information is provided.

When using an LLMs one can also follow up with a second prompt. If you do not trust the information provided, you can ask for clarification or call out the LLM directly. If you question a case citation made, ask about it.

Are those all actual cases?

Of course, you cannot trust the answer given. But sometimes, the LLM will reveal its mistake. It may have been a mistake in not understanding the context, or it may be what seems like an alarming hallucination that is difficult to understand.

I apologize for the confusion...

Another effective way of avoiding hallucination is:

...Consider this request step-by-step.

When you ask for an answer to be explained step-by-step, you often receive better results and have a better understanding of the reasoning used to arrive at the conclusion.

Another effective way of avoiding hallucination is:

...Provide reasoning supporting your answer.

## Role play

One useful strategy is to define a role of a specific persona or identity and instruct the large language model, such as ChatGPT to adopt it during the conversation or in performance of a particular task.

The API for OpenAI's ChatGPT model includes "role" as one of its parameters. This is a strong indicator that defining a role is important.

Different roles may use different language styles or vocabulary. For example, a poet would use different language than a physicist who would use different language than a lawyer. A poet might use more figurative language while an engineer might use more technical language and a lawyer might use more legal language. If one compares the writings of a poet, an engineer, and a lawyer, no doubt there are many more differences not just in vocabulary, but in structure, turn-of-phrase, and otherwise. There are differences which may be difficult for us to discern and express, but will be understandable to a large language model.

Also consider that many of us wear more than one hat, and sometimes at the same time. For example, as a patent attorney I am both a lawyer and an engineer. When assigning a role in your interactions with a large language model consider that we can be extremely specific about the role being performed or we may combine the role of multiple people into a single role.

This is one of the strengths of large language models which have been trained in numerous domains. So although perhaps I might write a better patent claim directed towards an electronics invention than ChatGPT can when instructed to take the role of a patent attorney, I cannot write as good of a patent claim in iambic pentameter as ChatGPT instructed to take the role of a patent attorney and poet. We can define a role in a manner even if there is no single person in the world who meets all of the qualifications we provide!

Act as a [insert role]

Of course, any number of roles may be used. This may include acting as a particular type of lawyer, acting as a judge, acting as a mediator, acting as a law professor, acting as an assistant, acting as a particular type of expert witness, or any other type of individual. Of course, the role assigned does not need to be human.

Your role is a legislative aid working for the Iowa legislature. Draft proposed legislation for the Transparency In Gratuities Act. The proposed legislation will require all establishments which promote payment of gratuities, including collecting gratuities from patrons through payment cards to prominently disclose who receives the direct benefit of any gratuity and any gratuity sharing arrangement if present. The proposed legislation will also require owners of establishments to prominently disclose whether employees who receive direct benefit from gratuities receive direct wages above or below minimum wage. These disclosures may be made on printed receipts or on electronic displays or posted so this information is readily available to patrons at time of any request for providing gratuities.

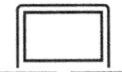

Bill No. [BILL NUMBER]

A Bill

For an Act relating to the disclosure of gratuity distribution and wage information at establishments that promote payment of gratuities; providing for penalties; and including effective date provisions.

Be It Enacted by the General Assembly of the State of Iowa:

Section 1. NEW SECTION. 123A.1 Title.

This Act shall be known and may be cited as the "Transparency In Gratuities Act."

Sec. 2. NEW SECTION. 123A.2 Definitions.

For purposes of this Act:

1.      "Establishment" means any business or venue that provides goods or services and promotes payment of gratuities by patrons, including, but not limited to, restaurants, bars, cafes, and hotels.

2.      "Gratuity" means a voluntary payment made by a patron in addition to the price of goods or services, as a token of appreciation for the service provided.

3.      "Owner" means any person, partnership, corporation, or other legal entity that operates or controls an establishment.

Sec. 3. NEW SECTION. 123A.3 Disclosure of gratuity distribution.

1.      An owner of an establishment shall prominently disclose the following information at the time of any request for providing gratuities:

a. The identity of the employee or employees who will receive the direct benefit of any gratuity provided by a patron.

b. If applicable, a description of any gratuity-sharing arrangement between employees, including the percentage or amount of gratuity each employee will receive.

2. The disclosure required under this section may be made through any of the following methods:

a. Printed on a customer's receipt.

b. Displayed on an electronic payment device or system used by patrons.

c. Posted in a conspicuous location within the establishment that is readily visible to patrons.

Sec. 4. NEW SECTION. 123A.4 Disclosure of wage information.

1. An owner of an establishment shall prominently disclose whether employees receive direct wages above or below the minimum wage.

2. The disclosure required under this section may be made through any of the following methods:

a. Printed on a customer's receipt.

b. Displayed on an electronic payment device or system used by patrons.

c. Posted in a conspicuous location within the establishment that is readily visible to patrons.

Sec. 5. NEW SECTION. 123A.5 Penalties.

1.      An owner of an establishment who fails to comply with the disclosure requirements of this Act shall be subject to a civil penalty not to exceed $500 for each violation.

2.      Each day an owner fails to comply with the disclosure requirements of this Act shall constitute a separate violation.

Sec. 6. EFFECTIVE DATE.

This Act, being deemed of immediate importance, shall take effect and be in force from and after its passage and publication.

Passed by the [Chamber], [Date].

Passed by the [Chamber], [Date].

Approved by the Governor, [Date].

---

Some uses of AI may involve replacing a team of individuals where each individual performs a specific task, and the AI framework feeds the output from one role to another role to yet another role. In these paradigms, each prompt to the AI is performing a different job role. Perhaps, that is an appropriate approach. It is easier for an individual to understand such an approach as it mimics how tasks might be performed in a group or an organization. However, in some instances better results may be obtained by including all of these separate roles into a single prompt and generating a single output. Such an approach also will be faster and perhaps cost less.

You are a team which includes a director of media communications, a director of public relations, a securities attorney, a tax attorney, an advertising attorney, and an intellectual property attorney. Please review the following draft tweet to be sent by the corporate CEO of a publicly traded company and comment on any potential legal or communications issues and a list of questions that should be answered or information confirmed before the CEO sends the tweet. Comments and questions should be integrated into a separate set of each and should not be divided by team member. Tweet: "Funding secured"

I. Comments on Potential Legal and Communications Issues:

1.      Securities law: The tweet may be considered market-moving information and could raise questions about whether it complies with the SEC's fair disclosure regulations (Regulation FD). The CEO should ensure that any material, non-public information is disclosed in a manner compliant with SEC regulations, avoiding selective disclosure or market manipulation.

2.      False or misleading statements: The CEO should verify that the statement "Funding secured" is accurate and not misleading. Misleading statements could expose the company and the CEO to liability under securities law, such as Rule 10b-5 of the Securities Exchange Act of 1934, and may potentially result in shareholder lawsuits.

3.      Advertising law: If the tweet could be interpreted as promoting the company's products or services, the CEO should ensure that the statement complies with relevant advertising laws and regulations, such as the Federal Trade Commission Act, which prohibits deceptive or unfair trade practices.

4.      Intellectual property: If the tweet contains any trademarks, copyrighted material, or other intellectual

property, the CEO should confirm that the company has the necessary rights or permissions to use such material.

5.     Public relations: The tweet may have significant public relations implications. The director of public relations should assess the potential impact of the tweet on the company's image and reputation, and advise the CEO on appropriate messaging strategies.

II. Questions and Information to Confirm Before Sending the Tweet:

1.     Has the funding referred to in the tweet been definitively secured, with all necessary agreements and approvals in place?

2.     Has the tweet been reviewed and approved by the company's legal counsel, particularly the securities attorney, to ensure compliance with all applicable laws and regulations?

3.     Are there any material details related to the funding that should be disclosed alongside the statement "Funding secured" in order to avoid providing a misleading or incomplete picture?

4.     Have any confidential or proprietary information been inadvertently included in the tweet, which could harm the company's competitive position or expose it to legal liability?

5.     Has the tweet been reviewed by the director of media communications and the director of public relations to ensure that the message is consistent with the company's broader communications strategy and objectives?

6.     Are there any upcoming events, announcements, or other developments that could influence the timing or content of the tweet, in order to maximize its positive impact and minimize any potential negative repercussions?

The Applications Programming Interface (API) for OpenAI allows one to specify a particular role for ChatGPT to have during a conversation. Thus, clearly, role is considered important and so is something you should often include within a prompt where assigning a specific role will result in better obtaining results consistent with that role.

The role you ask ChatGPT to take does not need to be generalized or fictious. You can ask ChatGPT to take on the role of a particular individual, whether it be a famous jurist like Learned Hand or a best-selling author.

## Style, tone, and audience

When a role is given, it often provides context relevant to style, tone, and audience. However, instead of specifying a role, style, tone, and/or audience may be specified instead.

Although style and tone are related, there are distinctions between style and tone. Style describes the way a message is structured and presented. This may involve word choice, sentence structure, and organization. Tone conveys the attitude or emotion behind the message.

Of course, there are many ways one can specify style, tone, and audience.

## *Style*

Please provide a list of words or expressions that may be used to specify different styles that a lawyer might use when prompt engineering.

➤ Analytical: A style that involves breaking down complex issues into smaller components and examining each part in detail.

➤ Persuasive: Using language, evidence, and logic to convince the audience of a particular viewpoint or course of action.

➤ Concise: Communicating the main points in a brief and clear manner, without excessive detail or redundancy.

➤ Narrative: Telling a story or presenting information in a chronological order to make it easier for the audience to follow and understand.

➤ Authoritative: Speaking with confidence and demonstrating a strong understanding of the law and relevant precedents to establish credibility.

➤ Empathetic: Demonstrating an understanding of and sensitivity to the emotions and experiences of the parties involved, in order to build rapport and trust.

> Socratic: Using a series of questions to guide the audience to a conclusion, allowing them to discover the answer for themselves.

> Jargon-free: Avoiding legal terminology and instead using plain, accessible language to make the information more easily understood by a lay audience.

> Collaborative: Working together with other parties, such as opposing counsel or mediators, to find common ground and reach a mutually acceptable resolution.

> Pragmatic: Focusing on practical solutions and considering the real-world consequences of legal decisions, rather than relying solely on abstract principles or theoretical arguments.

> Assertive: Clearly and confidently expressing one's position or opinion without being aggressive or confrontational.

> Logical: Presenting arguments in a structured and coherent manner, using reasoning and evidence to support each point.

> Adaptive: Adjusting the style of communication and argumentation based on the needs and preferences of the audience or the specific circumstances of the case.

➢ Creative: Using innovative approaches, analogies, or metaphors to explain complex legal concepts or to present new perspectives on the issue at hand.

➢ Diplomatic: Navigating delicate situations with tact and discretion, maintaining a professional and respectful tone even during contentious discussions.

➢ Informative: Providing comprehensive and accurate information in a clear and organized manner, ensuring the audience has a solid understanding of the topic.

➢ Inquisitive: Asking probing questions to gather information, clarify points, or challenge assumptions, demonstrating curiosity and a desire for a deeper understanding.

➢ Fact-based: Relying on objective data and verifiable evidence to support arguments, rather than relying on emotions or subjective opinions.

➢ Solution-oriented: Focusing on identifying and resolving issues or disputes, rather than dwelling on problems or assigning blame.

➢ Invitational: Encouraging open discussion and inviting feedback, creating an atmosphere of collaboration and mutual respect.

## *Tone*

Please provide a list of words or expressions that may be used to specify different tones that a lawyer might use when prompt engineering.

> Formal: Using professional language, proper grammar, and adhering to established conventions in order to convey a sense of seriousness and respect.

> Informal: Adopting a more casual and conversational tone, using colloquial expressions and everyday language to make the content more relatable and approachable.

> Friendly: Maintaining a warm and amiable tone, creating a sense of rapport and goodwill with the audience.

> Neutral: Remaining unbiased and objective, avoiding strong emotions or personal opinions in order to present a balanced perspective.

> Passionate: Expressing enthusiasm, conviction, and deep personal commitment to the subject matter, often using emotive language and a more intense tone.

> Calm: Speaking in a measured and composed manner, conveying a sense of steadiness and control even in high-pressure situations.

➢ Confident: Speaking with self-assurance and conviction, demonstrating a strong belief in the validity of one's arguments and expertise.

➢ Humble: Showing modesty and deference, acknowledging the limitations of one's knowledge or the complexities of the subject matter.

➢ Assertive: Clearly and firmly stating one's position or opinion, without being overly aggressive or confrontational.

➢ Dispassionate: Maintaining an emotionally detached and impartial tone, focusing on facts and evidence rather than personal feelings or opinions.

➢ Respectful: Demonstrating consideration and esteem for the opinions, feelings, and experiences of others, even when discussing contentious issues.

➢ Sincere: Speaking with genuine emotion and honesty, aiming to convey authenticity and credibility.

➢ Humorous: Using wit, jokes, or amusing anecdotes to lighten the mood and engage the audience, while still addressing the subject matter seriously.

➢ Ironical: Employing irony or sarcasm to make a point or highlight inconsistencies or contradictions in an argument.

➤ Inspirational: Using uplifting language and vivid imagery to motivate and encourage the audience, often appealing to their values or aspirations.

➤ Empathetic: Expressing understanding and compassion for the emotions and experiences of others, aiming to build rapport and trust.

➤ Intense: Using a heightened, dramatic tone to convey the urgency or gravity of the situation, often employing powerful language and vivid imagery.

➤ Diplomatic: Navigating sensitive topics or conflicts with tact and discretion, maintaining a professional and respectful tone.

➤ Questioning: Adopting a tone of inquiry or curiosity, encouraging the audience to reflect on their own beliefs and assumptions.

➤ Reassuring: Providing comfort and support, using a calm and soothing tone to alleviate concerns or anxieties.

### *Audience*

It can also be immensely helpful in establishing context to specify who the audience is for content generation or for editing content.

Draft a letter explaining what an [insert subject] is in a manner that someone with only an 8th grade education would understand.

Rewrite the following letter in a manner which is more natural sounding and appropriate for a medical doctor [letter].

## Length

Sometimes it is helpful to specify the length of the desired output, whether it is by number of words (e.g. 500), or number of sentences (one sentence), number of paragraphs, number of characters or some other understandable measure. If brainstorming or asking for a list, provide the number of items you would like to see.

Remember that there are context window limitations for the LLM, which include both the input and the output. Therefore, if you need help drafting a longer document, it may make sense to break it into smaller pieces and provide sufficient context for each piece of the document.

## Creativity

Due to the way that LLMs are constructed they can be more creative or more deterministic. If you would like to understand at a lower level, as previously explained, LLMs will predict the next token to generate in a statistical manner. However, there is variability in what token is selected next and two relevant parameters. The OpenAI API includes these additional parameters. These are "Temperature" and "Top_P". These parameters control the randomness and creativity of the text generated. The temperature values for the OpenAI API are between 0 and 1. A higher temperature value (e.g. 1.0) results in more randomness and creativity in the generated text while a lower temperature value (e.g. 0.1) will make the output more deterministic.

Top-p sampling is an alternative to temperature-based sampling where tokens are selected from the top-p of the probability distribution. As with temperature, a higher value of p (e.g. 1.0) will result in a more diverse and creative output while a lower value of (e.g. 0.1) will result in a more focused and deterministic output.

Putting statistics and the inner workings of a GPT models aside, the takeaway is that one can make LLMs more creative or less creative. If identifying facts, one may want the LLM to be less creative. When generating ideas, one may want the LLMs to be more creative. Where one does not have direct access to these parameters, one can construct their prompts in a manner to specify the level of creativity.

One can do this by specifying particular roles, tones, and style. In addition, one can enhance creativity by providing context such as by including language like:

➢ Brainstorm...

➢ Thinking out of the box...

➢ ...crazy ideas...

➤ Being creative...

➤ Being super innovative...

➤ Provide an unorthodox approach...

➤ Conceive a futuristic approach to...

➤ Dream up a groundbreaking idea for...

➤ Generate a list of original ideas...

➤ Propose a radical rethinking...

It can further be useful to combine multiple examples of this type of language into the prompt. Although seemingly redundant, it can make a difference on the level of creativity expressed.

## *Integration of principles into applications*

As further evidence of the importance of these ideas, consider the following screen display from Microsoft Bing. Here, the user interface allows one to select a tone, a format, and a length for their output.

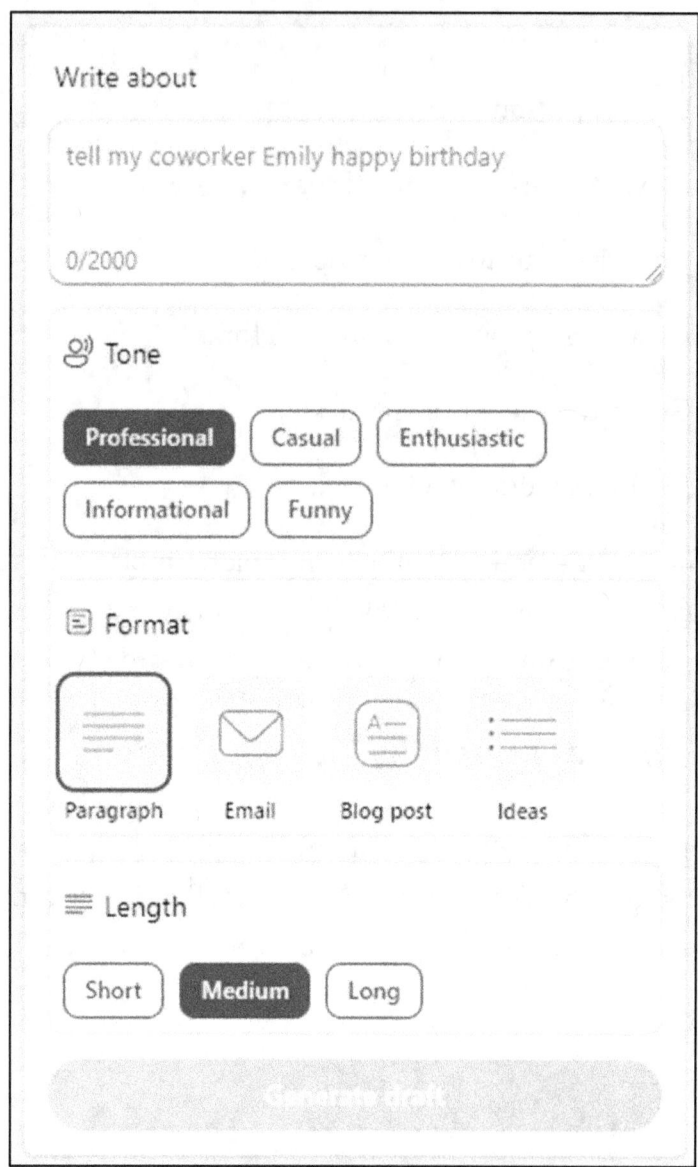

*Screenshot of Microsoft Bing. Copyright Microsoft Corporation*

The tone may be specified as professional, casual, enthusiastic, informational, or funny. The format may be specified as paragraph, email, blog post, or ideas, and the length may be specified as short, medium, or long.

We will see a growing number of similar approaches to help you use LLMs including interfaces specifically for lawyers to perform particular tasks.

# GOODHUE

CHAPTER FIVE

# Common uses

There is no end to the creativity you can express in order to obtain the desired results using an LLM. Here we describe some of the different actions associated with common use cases.

## *Generate*

Of course, one of the most common use cases for LLMs is to draft, create, write, or otherwise generate content such as text. This was shown in previous examples and will be shown in other examples throughout.

## *Revise*

Remember, however, that in addition to generating text, you can also use an LLM to edit, revise, or rewrite. Rewriting is a helpful tool in a number of different situations when one already has a writing, for example, a form letter but wants to adapt it to a different audience or to a different situation, in a different tone, or in a different style.

Please rewrite the following letter to suggest revisions to make the letter easier to understand, clearer, and to anticipate and address questions so that a client reading it may better understand. Information between curly brackets {} specifies form fields and should not be altered: [[letter omitted]].

Dear {Matter.ClientContact.First}:

We are pleased to inform you that the above application has been issued as United States Patent No. {Matter.PatentNum}, dated {Matter.IssueDate(MMMM d, yyyy)}. The original letters patent is enclosed. This patent protection is valid for a period of 20 years from the earliest non-provisional priority filing date of the patent. To provide notice to others and to protect your rights, we recommend that you display the patent number on the patented product and include it in all promotional literature relating to the patented product.

We have carefully proofread the patent for errors on the face of the document and within the claims, and we did not find any obvious errors.

Your patent has qualified for a patent term adjustment, which means that the Patent Office has added {Matter.PatentTermAdjustment(0)} days to the life of your patent. As a result, your patent will now expire on {Matter.ExpiredDate(MMMM d, yyyy)}, provided maintenance fees are paid in a timely manner. Please note that maintenance fees must be paid three times during the life of this patent: on the 3.5-, 7.5-, and 11.5-year anniversaries of the issue date. Failure to pay these fees by their respective deadlines will lead to early expiration of the patent.

## *Summarize*

Summarization is a type of action which LLMs can perform especially well. Whether asking to summarize a legal decision or a technical topic, this is a useful action to perform.

Please generate a brief one paragraph summary of Alice Corp. Pty. Ltd. v. CLS Bank International, 573 U.S. 208 (2014).

In Alice Corp. Pty. Ltd. v. CLS Bank International, 573 U.S. 208 (2014), the U.S. Supreme Court unanimously held that claims directed to an abstract idea, which merely required the implementation of a generic computer, were not patent-eligible under 35 U.S.C. § 101. The case involved a patent on a computer-implemented method for mitigating settlement risk in financial transactions. The Court applied the two-step framework established in Mayo Collaborative Services v. Prometheus Laboratories, Inc., first determining that the claims were directed to an abstract idea and then analyzing whether the claims contained an "inventive concept" sufficient to transform the abstract idea into a patent-eligible application. The Court concluded that the claims did not contain any inventive concept, as they merely required generic computer implementation, and thus were not eligible for patent protection.

You can also summarize your own documents.

Please review the following NDA and summarize the major provisions in a table. [[NDA omitted]]

Below is a table summarizing the major provisions

| Provision | Summary |
|-----------|---------|
| 1 | Defines "Confidential Information" as information disclosed by Discloser to Recipient, with specific conditions and exclusions. |
| 2 | Outlines Recipient's obligations in handling Confidential Information, including non-disclosure, limited use within their organization, protection, and returning materials upon termination of the agreement. Specifies notification requirements if legal disclosure is required. |
| 3 | Requires Recipient to notify Discloser of any unauthorized disclosure or use of Confidential Information and cooperate to prevent further unauthorized use. |

| 4 | Establishes that Discloser retains ownership of Confidential Information and all related Intellectual Property Rights. Recipient is not granted any rights to Confidential Information and is prohibited from seeking Intellectual Property Rights related to it. |
|---|---|
| 5 | States that the Agreement is the complete agreement between parties, can only be modified in writing, and that no waiver is implied by any act or failure to act. |
| 6 | Specifies the duration of the Agreement (three years) and the obligations of Recipient (five years from the first disclosure for most Confidential Information; indefinitely for trade secrets). |

## *Classify*

This is another action which is a classic use case for AIs. There are numerous instances where a lawyer may want to classify a case, a document, a client, a risk, or something else into one or more of a set of classifications.

Please classify the following potential trademarks for laundry detergent by distictivesness (generic, descriptive, suggestive, arbitrary, fanciful): Sparkles, Cleanly, Radzle, Laundry Magic, Detergent 2X.

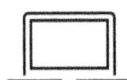

In Trademark distinctiveness is a key principle underlying trademark law. Here's how I would classify the proposed trademarks for a laundry detergent:

Sparkles: This could be seen as "suggestive." The term implies that the detergent will leave clothes sparkling clean, but it doesn't directly describe the product. Consumers would need to use some imagination to connect the term with the product.

Cleanly: This is likely "descriptive." It directly describes a desirable quality of the laundry detergent (that it cleans in a clean manner). Descriptive marks are not inherently distinctive and are only protected if they have acquired secondary meaning, indicating to consumers a unique source of the product.

Radzle: This appears to be a made-up word and would be classified as "fanciful." Fanciful trademarks are inherently distinctive and are afforded the strongest protection because they are invented words with no dictionary or common meaning.

Laundry Magic: This can be considered "suggestive." While it doesn't directly describe the product, it implies that the detergent has a 'magical' or extraordinary cleaning effect, requiring some imagination on the part of the consumer.

Detergent 2X: This would be "descriptive," as it directly describes a characteristic of the product (presumably that it's twice as effective or concentrated as regular detergent). Like "Cleanly," this type of trademark would require evidence of secondary meaning to be protected.

Remember, this is a general classification and the exact classification can depend on the context and how the trademarks are used in the market. In a real-world scenario, it would be best to consult with a trademark attorney or professional for advice.

## *Extract*

This is another action which can be helpful whether you are trying to extract legal citations, relevant facts, or other specific information from a document.

Extract all legal citations from the following document: [document text ommitted].

Extract all dates and times from the following document and generate a timeline indicating what occurred at each time [document text omitted].

## Sentiment analysis

Sentiment analysis involves analyzing people's sentiments, attitudes, opinions, and emotions from written language usually to better understand the attitude of the individual with respect to a particular document. It may also be used to detect subjectivity or objectivity or different emotional states and intensities.

Please comment on the sentiment expressed in the dissenting opinion in the Supreme Court case of West Virginia v. Environmental Protection Agency (2022)

The dissenting opinion in the Supreme Court case of West Virginia v. Environmental Protection Agency (2022) is largely one of anger and frustration. The dissenting justices, led by Justice Elena Kagan, argue that the majority opinion is "a breathtaking act of judicial overreach" that "will hamstring the Environmental Protection Agency's ability to protect the public from the existential threat of climate change."

The dissenting justices are particularly critical of the majority's use of the "major questions doctrine," which the majority uses to argue that the EPA does not have the authority to regulate greenhouse gas emissions from power plants. The dissenting justices argue that the major questions doctrine is a "novel and unprincipled" doctrine

71

that "has no basis in the text of the Constitution or our precedent."

The dissenting justices also argue that the majority's decision is "a betrayal of the public trust." They argue that the EPA is "the nation's premier environmental agency" and that it has a "critical role to play in protecting the public from the dangers of climate change." The dissenting justices argue that the majority's decision "will make it much more difficult for the EPA to do its job and protect the public from this existential threat."

The dissenting opinion in West Virginia v. Environmental Protection Agency is a powerful and passionate argument against the majority's decision. The dissenting justices make a strong case that the majority's decision is "a breathtaking act of judicial overreach" that will "hamstring the Environmental Protection Agency's ability to protect the public from the existential threat of climate change."

## *Translate*

This is another action which can be useful where you are translating from one language to another or where you are translating from one tone or style to another tone or style. You can also translate text from first person to second person or third person.

Please translate the following conversation into proper and complete English:

Teen 1: Hey, 📷 WYD?

Teen 2: Nm, 🐕 hbu?

Teen 1: Just 🤣 at some dank memes. BTW, 🙇 IDC what anyone says, YOLO, right? 💃

Teen 2: IKR? 🙇 Tbh, 👻 IDK why ppl get so salty. It's all just bants. 😌

Teen 1: Yeah, 🙄 FOMO is real tho. Don't wanna miss out on the tea. 💻

Teen 2: For sure, 😌 JOMO isn't for me. 🙇

Teen 1: Same, 🖥 I'm always on the TL, gotta keep up. 🙇 SMH at all the drama tho.

Teen 2: IKR, 🙀 can't even. But it's 🔥 lowkey lit too.

Teen 1: 🎯 On point. BTW, 🎮 GG on that test. Heard you aced it! 📑

Teen 2: 🙇 Tysm! 🏃 Gtg now, 🖥 TTYL?

Teen 1: ✌ Np, 📞 TTYL!

---

Teen 1: Hello, what are you doing?

Teen 2: Not much, what about you?

Teen 1: I'm just laughing at some really good memes. By the way, I don't care what anyone says, you only live once, right?

Teen 2: I know, right? To be honest, I don't know why people get so upset. It's all just friendly banter.

Teen 1: Yes, the fear of missing out is real though. I don't want to miss out on the latest gossip.

Teen 2: For sure, the joy of missing out isn't for me.

Teen 1: Same here, I'm always checking my social media timeline, I have to keep up. But I do shake my head at all the drama.

Teen 2: I know, right? I can't even handle it. But it's subtly exciting too.

Teen 1: You're right. By the way, good job on that test. I heard you did very well!

Teen 2: Thank you so much! I have to go now, talk to you later?

Teen 1: No problem, talk to you later!

## *Analyze logic*

Another use of ChatGPT is to identify errors in logic or reliance on logical fallacies in arguments, whether your own or someone else's.

The following text is a part of an Examiner's Answer to an Appeal Brief where the Examiner is contending that claims of a patent application are obvious. Please review and identify any logical fallacies or errors in logical reasoning made by the Examiner. [[text omitted]].

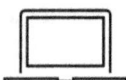

One logical fallacy in the Examiner's argument is the straw man fallacy. The Examiner misrepresents the Appellant's argument by claiming that they argue that the Examiner did not identify what claim elements are missing from references, combinations of references. However, the Appellant's argument is that the Examiner did not provide a clear articulation of why the invention would be obvious.

Another logical fallacy is the red herring fallacy. The Examiner argues that the exact language of Smith should not matter, but what is derived from the teaching. However, the Appellant's argument was not about the language but about the lack of teaching in Smith about the particular limitation.

Lastly, the Examiner's response to the argument that they did not properly determine the scope and contents of the prior art is insufficient. The Examiner simply states that this has been addressed fully somewhere else, without actually addressing it in the current argument.

## Idea generation

Another common use of LLMs is for idea generation or brainstorming.

What are 10 creative winning themes a plaintiff might use in a defamation case?

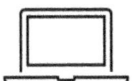

Defamation cases can be complex and often rely on the unique facts and circumstances surrounding the alleged defamation. Therefore, the precise themes a plaintiff might use can vary significantly. However, here are 10 general themes that could be effective in a defamation case:

1.      Truth and Integrity: Emphasize the plaintiff's character and reputation for honesty and integrity, underscoring the damage caused by the defamatory statements.

2.      Dignity and Respect: Highlight the importance of treating people with dignity and respect, and how the defamatory statements violated these principles.

3.      The Power of Words: Discuss the power and influence of words and communication, and how they can be misused to cause harm.

4.    The Ripple Effect: Describe the wider impacts of defamation, such as the effects on family, friends, and colleagues.

5.    Accountability: Stress the need for the defendant to take responsibility for their actions and the harm they caused.

6.    The Impact on Future Opportunities: Explain how the defamation can have long-term impacts, such as future job prospects or social opportunities.

7.    Malice or Negligence: If applicable, emphasize the defendant's malicious intent or negligence in making the false statements.

8.    The Importance of Reputation: Discuss how hard it is to build a good reputation and how easily it can be destroyed.

9.    Freedom of Speech vs. Responsibility: While freedom of speech is important, it's equally important to use that freedom responsibly and not to harm others.

10.    The Role of the Internet and Social Media: Discuss the role that digital platforms can play in spreading defamatory statements and exacerbating their impacts.

Remember, the plaintiff's attorney must carefully tailor these themes to the specific facts and circumstances of the case. The law surrounding defamation can be complex and varies between jurisdictions, so it's crucial to consult with a legal professional when dealing with potential defamation issues.

# CHAPTER SIX

# Form of output

One can prompt a LLM to provide output in a desired form. This can often be a powerful and useful approach. There are numerous contexts where this is helpful.

## *Lists and Outlines*

Lists and outlines are often useful ways or receiving output. Many times without specifically prompting, output will be provided in numbered format. However, you can specify whether you want a "list" or "outline" in order to have the output returned in the format you want. Sometimes this can be incredibly useful when you want to use the output in another application. The following example uses an outline from an LLM to bootstrap a Microsoft PowerPoint presentation.

I want to create a PowerPoint presentation on making takedown complaints to social media, app store, and ecommerce web sites. The presentation should be targeted towards lawyers and should disclose the processes involved as well as suggestions for being more successful in having infringing content removed per the policies of the particular web sites. Please provide an outline to cut and paste into PowerPoint and to use to create slides using the "Slides from Outline" feature of PowerPoint. This will be a 30 minute presentation.

```
css

I. Introduction
   A. Overview of the presentation
   B. Importance of addressing online infringement

II. Understanding Takedown Complaints
   A. What is a takedown complaint?
   B. Legal basis for takedown complaints
      1. Digital Millennium Copyright Act (DMCA)
      2. Trademark infringement
      3. Other legal grounds

III. Takedown Complaints on Social Media Platforms
   A. Overview of popular social media platforms
   B. Process for submitting takedown complaints on social med:
      1. Identifying infringing content
      2. Submitting a complaint through online forms
      3. Follow-up and resolution
   C. Tips for successful takedown complaints on social media
      1. Provide clear and accurate information
      2. Understand the platform's policies
      3. Monitor for repeat infringement
```

The result from this prompt includes text in the form of an outline which may then be saved as a text file, such as by copying and pasting into a text file in Notepad or another text editor and saving the file, e.g. **outline.txt**. Once the file is saved,

➢ Open Microsoft PowerPoint and create a new presentation.

➢ Select the "Home" tab in the ribbon.

➢ In the "Slides" group, click on the "New Slide" drop-down arrow.

> ➤ From the drop-down menu, select "Slides from Outline".

> ➤ In the "Insert Outline" dialog box, navigate to the location of the text file you just created (e.g. outline.txt).

> ➤ Select the file and click "Insert".

The results in creating a set of slides as shown below.

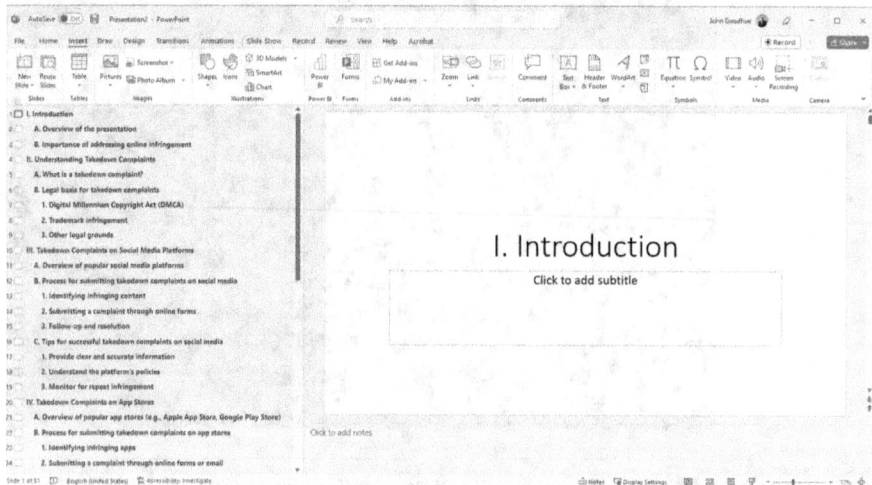

Thus, not only can you quickly create an outline, albeit a generic one in this instance, you can quickly create an outline in a format which facilitates quickly creating a slide set. Of course, you can edit the outline in the text file before you generate your slides.

## *Table*

There are many instances where it is helpful to generate output in a table format with desired columns and rows. This is especially useful if the output data is to be copied and pasted to another application such as Microsoft Excel or Google Sheets, or just to keep the results organized.

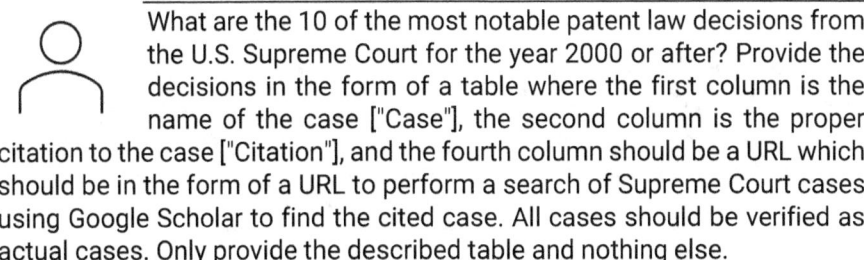

What are the 10 of the most notable patent law decisions from the U.S. Supreme Court for the year 2000 or after? Provide the decisions in the form of a table where the first column is the name of the case ["Case"], the second column is the proper citation to the case ["Citation"], and the fourth column should be a URL which should be in the form of a URL to perform a search of Supreme Court cases using Google Scholar to find the cited case. All cases should be verified as actual cases. Only provide the described table and nothing else.

| Case | Citation | URL |
| --- | --- | --- |
| Festo Corp. v. Shoketsu Kinzoku Kogyo Kabushiki Co. | 535 U.S. 722 (2002) | Festo Corp. v. Shoketsu Kinzoku Kogyo Kabushiki Co. |
| Merck KGaA v. Integra Lifesciences I, Ltd. | 545 U.S. 193 (2005) | Merck KGaA v. Integra Lifesciences I, Ltd. |
| eBay Inc. v. MercExchange, L.L.C. | 547 U.S. 388 (2006) | eBay Inc. v. MercExchange, L.L.C. |
| KSR International Co. v. Teleflex Inc. | 550 U.S. 398 (2007) | KSR International Co. v. Teleflex Inc. |
| Bilski v. Kappos | 561 U.S. 593 (2010) | Bilski v. Kappos |

| Case | Citation | URL |
|---|---|---|
| Mayo Collaborative Services v. Prometheus Laboratories, Inc. | 566 U.S. 66 (2012) | Mayo Collaborative Services v. Prometheus Laboratories, Inc. |
| Ass'n for Molecular Pathology v. Myriad Genetics, Inc. | 569 U.S. 576 (2013) | Ass'n for Molecular Pathology v. Myriad Genetics, Inc. |
| Alice Corp. Pty. Ltd. v. CLS Bank International | 573 U.S. 208 (2014) | Alice Corp. Pty. Ltd. v. CLS Bank International |
| Kimble v. Marvel Entertainment, LLC | 576 U.S. 446 (2015) | Kimble v. Marvel Entertainment, LLC |
| Cuozzo Speed Technologies, LLC v. Lee | 579 U.S. 261 (2016) | Cuozzo Speed Technologies, LLC v. Lee |
| Impression Products, Inc. v. Lexmark International, Inc. | 581 U.S. 1523 (2017) | Impression Products, Inc. v. Lexmark International, Inc. |

Here, we specifically stated the different columns we want for the table.

## Links

Note that in the above example, links were also produced in the table which is possible even with a LLM that is not able to access or search the Internet. Here, the links produced are possible because it understands the format for performing a search in Google Scholar. The links here are not directly to the particular case but to search results in Google Scholar searching for the cases.

The same type of approach may be used to include links to searches performed in Google, Bing, or other search engines, even if the LLM does not have the ability to browse the internet.

## *Checklists*

Another often useful type of output is output in the form of checklists, a specific type of list.

Generate a check list for filing a U.S. patent application by U.S. postal express email. Only include the checklist and nothing else. Preface each item with a box which can be checked.

☐ Completed and signed Application Data Sheet (ADS)

☐ Specification, including: ☐ Title of the invention ☐ Field of the invention ☐ Background of the invention ☐ Summary of the invention ☐ Brief description of the drawings (if applicable) ☐ Detailed description of the invention ☐ Abstract of the disclosure

☐ Claims, including: ☐ At least one independent claim ☐ Any dependent claims (if applicable)

☐ Drawings (if applicable): ☐ Each sheet of drawings properly labeled and numbered ☐ Brief description of each drawing ☐ Compliance with USPTO drawing standards

☐ Oath or Declaration: ☐ Properly executed by the inventor(s) ☐ Identifying the inventor(s) by full legal name(s) ☐ Including a statement of inventorship

☐ Appropriate filing fees: ☐ Basic filing fee ☐ Search fee ☐ Examination fee ☐ Any additional fees (e.g., for extra claims or multiple dependent claims)

☐ Cover letter, including: ☐ Correspondence address ☐ Contact information (telephone number and email address)

☐ Application type (e.g., utility, design, or plant) ☐ List of enclosed documents and fees

☐ Proper packaging and mailing: ☐ Addressed to the United States Patent and Trademark Office ☐ Sent via U.S. Postal Service Express Mail ☐ Correct postage affixed

☐ Optional items, if applicable: ☐ Information Disclosure Statement (IDS) ☐ Request for expedited examination under the Track One program ☐ Any required government or institutional forms (e.g., for federally funded research)

## *Markup*

By default ChatGPT may not provide proper formatting. For example, in a previous example of summarizing a case, the case name was not formatted properly either in the input or the output. You do not need to be content with unformatted output. Instead you can specify that proper formatting is added.

Please generate a brief one paragraph summary of Alice Corp. Pty. Ltd. v. CLS Bank International, 573 U.S. 208 (2014). Maintain proper formatting including for case names.

In the landmark decision of *Alice Corp. Pty. Ltd. v. CLS Bank International*, 573 U.S. 208 (2014), the U.S. Supreme Court unanimously held that Alice Corp.'s patent claims, which covered a computer-implemented method for mitigating settlement risk by using a third-party intermediary, were invalid because they were directed to an abstract idea, a fundamental economic practice. The Court clarified the two-step framework for determining patent eligibility under 35 U.S.C. § 101, first by identifying whether the claims are directed to an abstract idea, law of nature, or natural phenomenon, and then determining whether the claims

> contain an "inventive concept" that transforms the abstract idea into a patent-eligible invention. This decision has had a significant impact on patent law, particularly in the areas of software and business method patents.

Note that despite making the same request as before regarding the summary, a different output is produced. This is the nature of LLMs.

Google Bard even includes a feature where you may view multiple drafts of output and choose the version you prefer, so you do not need to submit the same prompt to see alternative versions of responses.

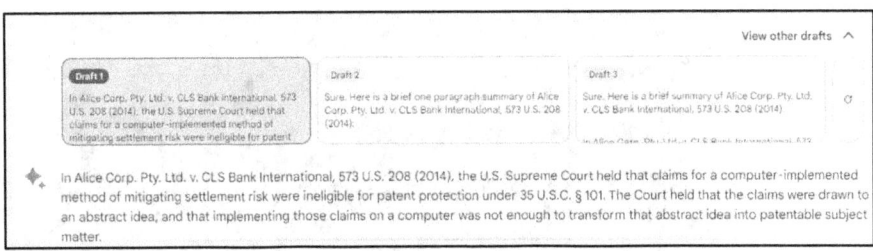

*Screenshot of Google Bard. Copyright Google LLC.*

## Code

In some instances it is helpful to generate an output as code. LLMs are being used by software developers to generate, explain, or edit code in order to increase efficiency. Although you certainly do not need to learn to code to use LLMs, if you already know how to, there are many new possibilities available to you.

It is also worthwhile to consider there are many different types of file formats which can be considered code. You can increase the capability of LLMs by asking it to generate code in the desired format. The following are some examples.

### *Flowchart*

LLMs are often eager to please and so if you ask for a flowchart you will receive one.

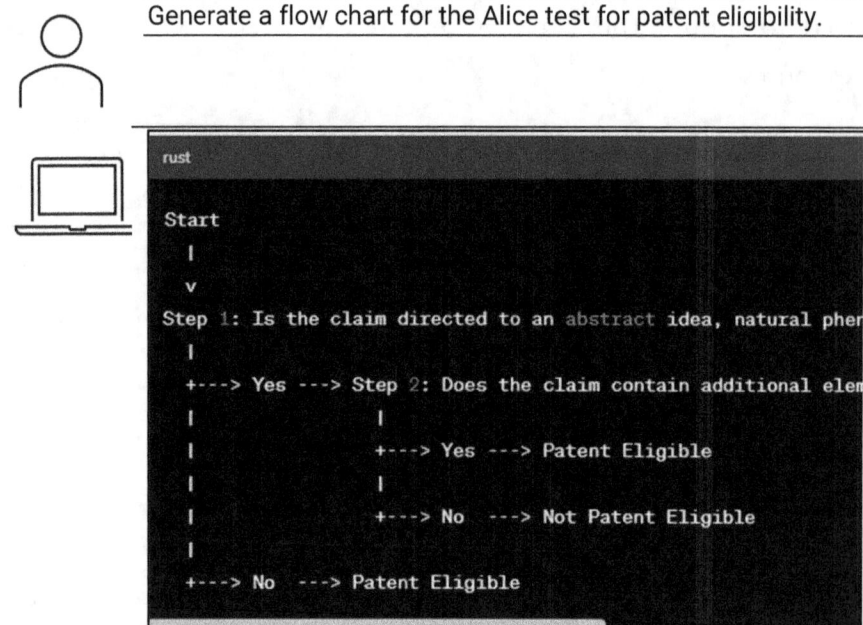

In the above example, an ASCII text flowchart was created. Although it is a flow chart and perhaps useful, it is not very attractive. It is worthwhile to note, however, that the LLM was not instructed regarding the logic of the flowchart but rather determined the structure from the relevant case.

But what if wanted a graphical flowchart and not a text one? Some LLMs may indicate that they cannot construct a graphical flow chart or other such output. However, if you ask in the proper manner, perhaps the LLM can. For example, you can ask it to generate the code for a flowchart which you can then save and open in an appropriate manner resulting in a flowchart.

Generate SVG code for a flow chart for the Alice test for patent eligibility.

```
<svg xmlns="http://www.w3.org/2000/svg" width="800" height="300" viewBox="0 0 800 300">

    <rect x="50" y="20" width="700" height="40" fill="white" stroke="black" />

    <text x="60" y="45" font-family="Arial" font-size="14">Step 1: Is the claim directed to an abstract idea, natural phenomenon, or law of nature?</text>

    <line x1="400" y1="60" x2="400" y2="80" stroke="black" />

    <text x="350" y="95" font-family="Arial" font-size="14">Yes</text>

    <text x="600" y="95" font-family="Arial" font-size="14">No</text>

    <rect x="100" y="100" width="600" height="40" fill="white" stroke="black" />

    <text x="110" y="125" font-family="Arial" font-size="14">Step 2: Does the claim contain additional elements that transform the nature of the claim into a patent-eligible application?</text>
```

```
<line x1="200" y1="140" x2="200" y2="160" stroke="black"
/>

<line x1="600" y1="140" x2="600" y2="160" stroke="black"
/>

<text    x="150"    y="175"    font-family="Arial"    font-
size="14">Yes</text>

<text    x="550"    y="175"    font-family="Arial"    font-
size="14">No</text>

  <rect x="125" y="180" width="150" height="40" fill="white"
stroke="black" />

<text    x="180"    y="205"    font-family="Arial"    font-
size="14">Patent Eligible</text>

  <rect x="525" y="180" width="150" height="40" fill="white"
stroke="black" />

<text    x="555"    y="205"    font-family="Arial"    font-
size="14">Not Patent Eligible</text>

</svg>
```

In the above example we asked for SVG code to be generated. SVG code is scalable vector graphics which is a file format based on XML which can be displayed in web browsers and other software. Like html or XML there are a series of tags that define an output, in this instance a graphic.

If the above code is saved to a text file such as by copying and pasting it into Notepad and then saving it to a file with a svg extension (such as flowchart.svg), it can then be inserted into a document as a picture or image or opened in a web browser. The resulting flow chart looks like this.

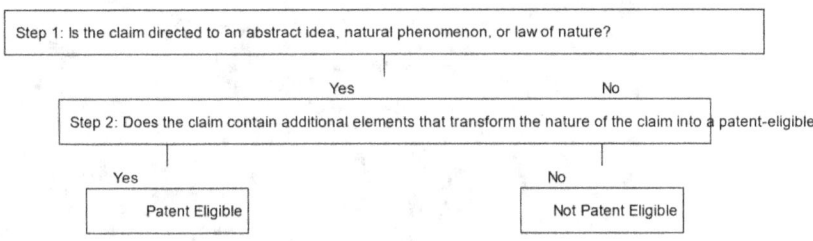

There are some clear errors in that the lines do not connect the boxes and the text for step 2 is not fully contained within the rectangle, but the image (or its code) could be modified, or the prompt may be altered to obtain improved results. Or alternatively, the file can be edited within a graphics program to address these errors.

Please generate JavaScript for a flow chart for the Alice test for patent eligibility using Mermaid.js. If any line of text in the flow chart is over 40 characters, split the line of text or shorten it.

```
html

<!DOCTYPE html>
<html>
<head>
  <title>Alice Test Flowchart</title>
  <script src="https://cdn.jsdelivr.net/npm/mermaid/dist/mermaid
</head>
<body>
  <div class="mermaid">
    graph TD
      st(Start)
      op1{Step 1: Is the claim directed<br>to an abstract idea,
      op2{Step 2: Does the claim<br>include an inventive<br>cond
      e1(Patent-Eligible)
      e2(Not Patent-Eligible)
      st --> op1
      op1 -->|Yes| op2
      op1 -->|No| e1
      op2 -->|Yes| e1
      op2 -->|No| e2
  </div>

  <script>
    // Initialize the Mermaid.js library
    mermaid.initialize({startOnLoad: true});
  </script>
</body>
</html>
```

↻ Regenerate response

The code generated in this example is for JavaScript which is within an HTML file which can be read by web browsers.

As before, we can save the code to an .html file such as by opening Notepad or another text editor, copying and pasting the code into our text editor and saving the file as **flowchart.html**. We can then open the **flowchart.html** in our web browser and we have the following flowchart.

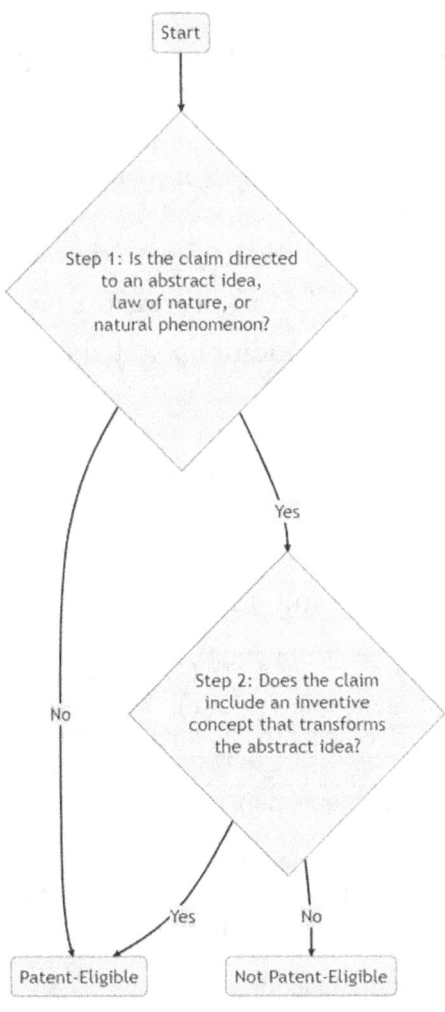

There are many situations where ChatGPT may not be able to perform a certain function directly, but it can help do so indirectly by creating code which when executed will perform the function.

In the above examples, the code was in the form of SVG code and HTML code with JavaScript. If you are familiar with python, JavaScript, Visual Basic script, or some other coding language, you have many more opportunities to leverage output to perform particular actions.

### *Equations*

Another special case is the representation of equations. You could, for example, ask an LLM to provide the integral form of Ampere's Law with Maxwell's Additions and the LLM would provide in substance:

$\oint B \cdot dl = \mu_0 I\_enclosed + \mu_0\varepsilon_0(d\Phi\_E/dt)$.

However, this is not formatted as one might want an equation to be. Here, there is a work around by asking for code.

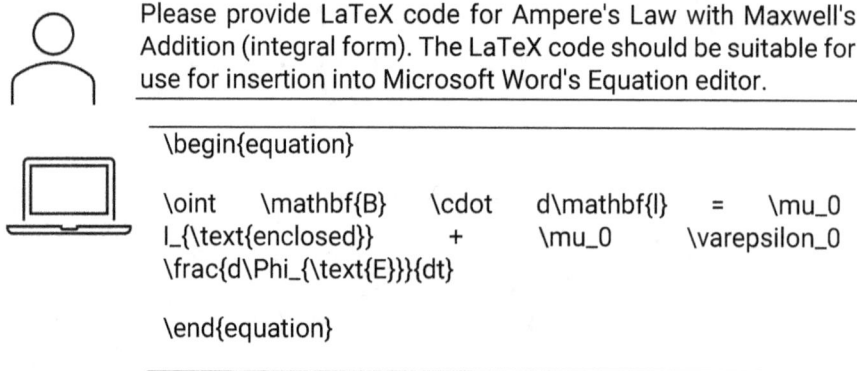

Please provide LaTeX code for Ampere's Law with Maxwell's Addition (integral form). The LaTeX code should be suitable for use for insertion into Microsoft Word's Equation editor.

```
\begin{equation}

\oint   \mathbf{B}   \cdot   d\mathbf{l}   =   \mu_0
I_{\text{enclosed}}   +   \mu_0   \varepsilon_0
\frac{d\Phi_{\text{E}}}{dt}

\end{equation}
```

In Microsoft Word, one can select to insert an equation and paste the LaTeX code in the Equation Editor to produce the equation, resulting in the following:

$$\oint \vec{B} \cdot d\vec{l} = \mu_0 I_{\text{enclosed}} + \mu_0 \varepsilon_0 \frac{d\Phi_E}{dt}$$

Note that in the above example additional context was provided in the prompt, namely, the context included how the results were going to be used. Here, this was important because LaTeX code may be formatted differently for different purposes, and this allows the LLM to get it right the first time and provide beautiful equations quickly.

## *Rich Text Format*

Another way to format text is to prompt an LLM such as ChatGPT to generate code for a Rich Text Format (RTF) file. This type of marked-up text file can be easily read by word processors such as Microsoft Word. This allows formatting beyond what a typical prompt output provides.

Generate code for an RTF file which includes a legal caption for Smith V. Johns which is a civil case in the Iowa District Court in Dallas County, Iowa.

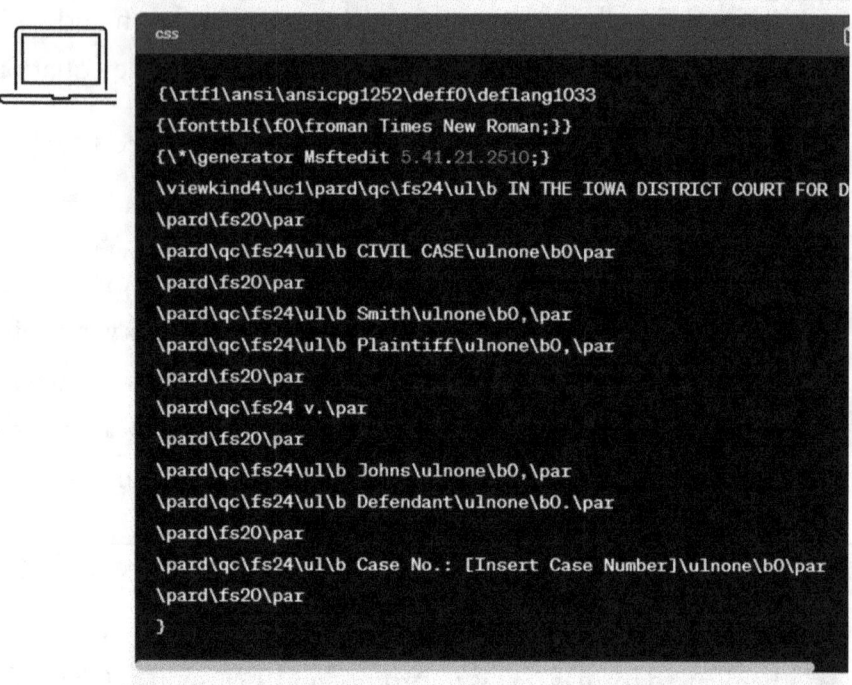

```
css

{\rtf1\ansi\ansicpg1252\deff0\deflang1033
{\fonttbl{\f0\froman Times New Roman;}}
{\*\generator Msftedit 5.41.21.2510;}
\viewkind4\uc1\pard\qc\fs24\ul\b IN THE IOWA DISTRICT COURT FOR D
\pard\fs20\par
\pard\qc\fs24\ul\b CIVIL CASE\ulnone\b0\par
\pard\fs20\par
\pard\qc\fs24\ul\b Smith\ulnone\b0,\par
\pard\qc\fs24\ul\b Plaintiff\ulnone\b0,\par
\pard\fs20\par
\pard\qc\fs24 v.\par
\pard\fs20\par
\pard\qc\fs24\ul\b Johns\ulnone\b0,\par
\pard\qc\fs24\ul\b Defendant\ulnone\b0.\par
\pard\fs20\par
\pard\qc\fs24\ul\b Case No.: [Insert Case Number]\ulnone\b0\par
\pard\fs20\par
}
```

You will then want to "Copy Code" to place it on the clipboard and then paste it into Notepad or another text editor. Next, save it as caption.rtf. Then open the RTF file in Microsoft Word.

**IN THE IOWA DISTRICT COURT FOR DALLAS COUNTY**

**CIVIL CASE**

**Smith,**
**Plaintiff,**

v.

**Johns,**
**Defendant.**

**Case No.: [Insert Case Number]**

Although the caption is not in the format desired, several types of formatting were applied including all caps, bold, underline, and centering.

But why be content with just a caption if we can have a complete shell document created?

Generate code for an RTF file which will serve as a shell for an appeal brief to be filed before the Patent Trial and Appeal Board to appeal a final rejection. The shell should have all the required headings.

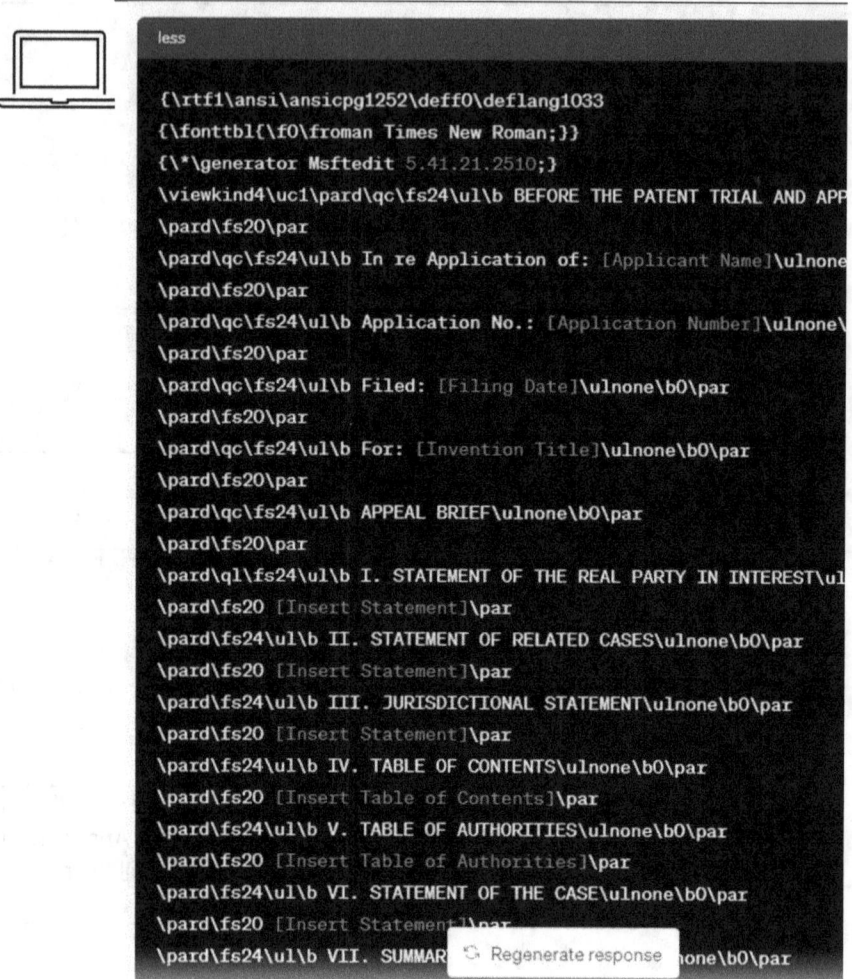

```
less

{\rtf1\ansi\ansicpg1252\deff0\deflang1033
{\fonttbl{\f0\froman Times New Roman;}}
{\*\generator Msftedit 5.41.21.2510;}
\viewkind4\uc1\pard\qc\fs24\ul\b BEFORE THE PATENT TRIAL AND APP
\pard\fs20\par
\pard\qc\fs24\ul\b In re Application of: [Applicant Name]\ulnone
\pard\fs20\par
\pard\qc\fs24\ul\b Application No.: [Application Number]\ulnone\
\pard\fs20\par
\pard\qc\fs24\ul\b Filed: [Filing Date]\ulnone\b0\par
\pard\fs20\par
\pard\qc\fs24\ul\b For: [Invention Title]\ulnone\b0\par
\pard\fs20\par
\pard\qc\fs24\ul\b APPEAL BRIEF\ulnone\b0\par
\pard\fs20\par
\pard\ql\fs24\ul\b I. STATEMENT OF THE REAL PARTY IN INTEREST\ul
\pard\fs20 [Insert Statement]\par
\pard\fs24\ul\b II. STATEMENT OF RELATED CASES\ulnone\b0\par
\pard\fs20 [Insert Statement]\par
\pard\fs24\ul\b III. JURISDICTIONAL STATEMENT\ulnone\b0\par
\pard\fs20 [Insert Statement]\par
\pard\fs24\ul\b IV. TABLE OF CONTENTS\ulnone\b0\par
\pard\fs20 [Insert Table of Contents]\par
\pard\fs24\ul\b V. TABLE OF AUTHORITIES\ulnone\b0\par
\pard\fs20 [Insert Table of Authorities]\par
\pard\fs24\ul\b VI. STATEMENT OF THE CASE\ulnone\b0\par
\pard\fs20 [Insert Statement]\par
\pard\fs24\ul\b VII. SUMMAR      Regenerate response   one\b0\par
```

As before, you can "Copy Code" to place it on the clipboard and then paste it into Notepad or another text editor. Next, save it as shell.rtf. Then open the RTF file in Microsoft Word.

**BEFORE THE PATENT TRIAL AND APPEAL BOARD**

**In re Application of: [Applicant Name]**

**Application No.: [Application Number]**

**Filed: [Filing Date]**

**For: [Invention Title]**

**APPEAL BRIEF**

**I. STATEMENT OF THE REAL PARTY IN INTEREST**
[Insert Statement]
**II. STATEMENT OF RELATED CASES**
[Insert Statement]
**III. JURISDICTIONAL STATEMENT**
[Insert Statement]
**IV. TABLE OF CONTENTS**
[Insert Table of Contents]
**V. TABLE OF AUTHORITIES**
[Insert Table of Authorities]
**VI. STATEMENT OF THE CASE**
[Insert Statement]
**VII. SUMMARY OF THE INVENTION**
[Insert Summary]
**VIII. ARGUMENT**
[Insert Argument]
**IX. CONCLUSION**
[Insert Conclusion]
**X. CLAIMS APPENDIX**
[Insert Claims Appendix]
**XI. CERTIFICATE OF COMPLIANCE**
[Insert Certificate of Compliance]
**XII. CERTIFICATE OF SERVICE**
[Insert Certificate of Service]

Here, without little prompting, the LLM determined the various parts of the Appeal Brief and included them. As within the previous example, bold, underline, all uppercase, and centering were applied. By further iterating the prompt, one could enhance the document generated.

GOODHUE

# CHAPTER SEVEN

# Training and simulation

Another powerful use of LLMs is in education, training, and simulation. Of course, one can use LLM to learn information. However, LLMs with conversational Ais such as ChatGPT can adopt a role for a series of interactions with a user in order to assist the lawyer in learning or practicing.

## *Anticipate objections training (preparation for court)*

You are an opposing attorney. I am an attorney asking questions of a witness. I will ask a question. If there is an objection under the federal rules, you will object by stating

99

"Objection." and then state the basis of the objection. If there is no objection, you will answer, "None".

Understood. Go ahead and ask your question.

State your name for the record.

None.

What happened after you recklessly changed lanes?

Objection. Assumes facts not in evidence (that the witness recklessly changed lanes).

## Constitutional law training (preparation for job interview)

You have probably often wondered how you might prepare for your confirmation hearing after your nomination to the U.S. Supreme Court.

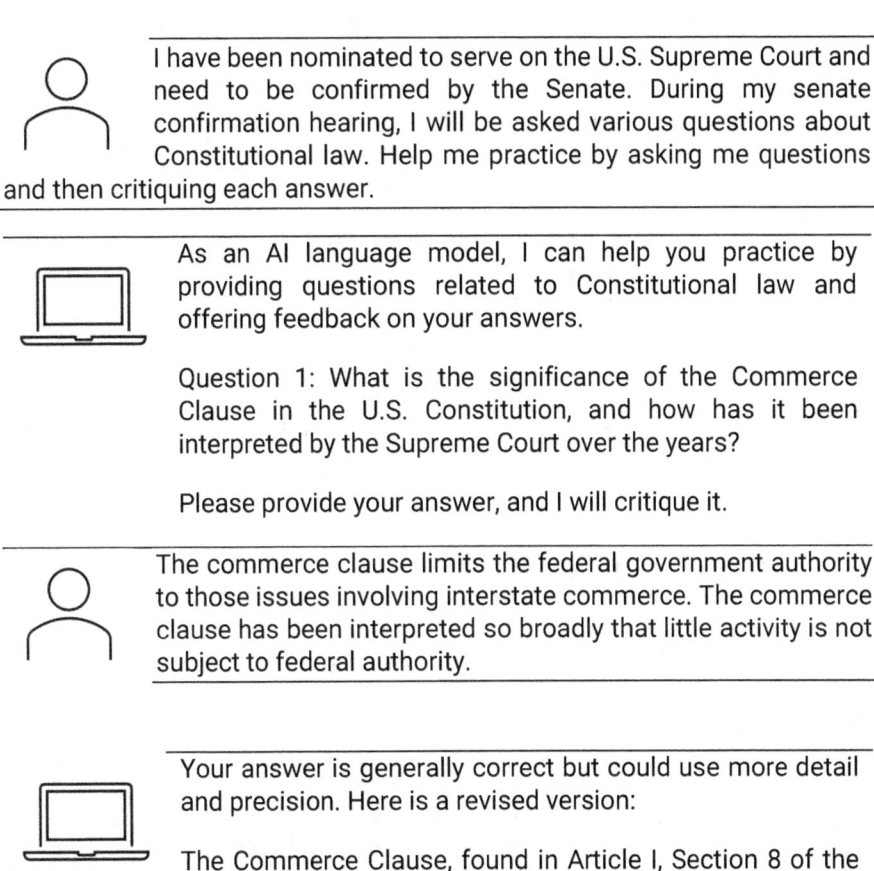

I have been nominated to serve on the U.S. Supreme Court and need to be confirmed by the Senate. During my senate confirmation hearing, I will be asked various questions about Constitutional law. Help me practice by asking me questions and then critiquing each answer.

As an AI language model, I can help you practice by providing questions related to Constitutional law and offering feedback on your answers.

Question 1: What is the significance of the Commerce Clause in the U.S. Constitution, and how has it been interpreted by the Supreme Court over the years?

Please provide your answer, and I will critique it.

The commerce clause limits the federal government authority to those issues involving interstate commerce. The commerce clause has been interpreted so broadly that little activity is not subject to federal authority.

Your answer is generally correct but could use more detail and precision. Here is a revised version:

The Commerce Clause, found in Article I, Section 8 of the U.S. Constitution, grants Congress the authority "to regulate Commerce with foreign Nations, and among the several States, and with the Indian Tribes." The clause plays a significant role in defining the scope of federal government power, particularly concerning economic activities.

> Over the years, the Supreme Court has interpreted the Commerce Clause in various ways. Initially, the Court took a more restrictive view, limiting federal authority to the regulation of activities directly related to interstate commerce. However, during the New Deal era, the Court shifted to a broader interpretation, allowing Congress to regulate any activities that had a substantial effect on interstate commerce, even if the activities themselves were local in nature. This expanded interpretation has been maintained in more recent cases, although the Court has occasionally set limits on Congress's authority under the Commerce Clause, such as in the cases of United States v. Lopez (1995) and United States v. Morrison (2000).
>
> Remember to provide historical context and specific case examples when discussing Supreme Court interpretations of the Constitution.

Of course, similar types of prompts may be used in any number of different situations, so there is no need to wait for your nomination to try it.

## *Learning technology*

LLMs such as ChatGPT can also be especially effective to learn technology.

> You are a trainer for Fastcase (https://www.fastcase.com/faq/). You will generate an example of a research question and then ask me to provide a Fastcase search strategy to address the research question. Then you will provide feedback and corrections to my Fastcase search strategy.

Sure, let's go through this process.

Research Question: "You are a lawyer working on a case that involves a dispute over water rights in the state of Colorado. You need to find case law that discusses similar disputes, specifically focusing on cases that have happened in the last 20 years. Moreover, you are interested in any cases where the rights of Indigenous communities were a factor."

Fastcase Search Strategy: Now, can you provide a Fastcase search strategy to address this research question?

I would select a State Jurisdiction of Colorado. I would provide a date range for the last 20 years. I would search for "water rights" AND ("indigenous" or "native american")

That's a great start! Your selection of the jurisdiction and date range is spot on. Your keyword search is well thought out, too. However, there are a few suggestions that could enhance the effectiveness of your search.

1.      **Phrase Searching**: Instead of searching "water rights" as separate keywords, you can use quotation marks to search for the exact phrase "water rights". This way, you ensure that your results are about water rights, rather than any results that just happen to contain both "water" and "rights" anywhere in the text.

2.      **Boolean Operators**: Your use of AND and OR operators is correct, but remember that Fastcase, like many other databases, reads boolean operators from left to right. This means that the current search might not work as you expect. It might be interpreted as searching for documents that contain both "water rights" and "indigenous", or documents that contain "native american". To get the results you want, you should use parentheses to group your

103

OR terms together: "water rights" AND ("indigenous" OR "native american").

3.      **Expanding the Search**: Consider including related terms, such as "tribal" or specific tribe names if you know them. This can help to ensure that you're not missing relevant cases. Also, consider the legal jargon that might be used in these cases. Instead of or in addition to "water rights", terms like "riparian rights" or "appropriative rights" might be used.

4.      **Using the NOT operator**: If there are any terms that you definitely do not want to appear in your results, you can use the NOT operator. For instance, if you were only interested in cases where the indigenous communities' rights were upheld, you could add NOT "rights denied" to your search.

So, your revised search strategy might look like this:

Jurisdiction: Colorado Date Range: Last 20 years Search: "water rights" OR "riparian rights" OR "appropriative rights" AND ("indigenous" OR "native american" OR "tribal") NOT "rights denied"

Remember, legal research can often involve a bit of trial and error, as well as refining your search terms based on the results you get. So, it's always a good idea to start broad and then narrow down as you review your results.

There are countless ways one can use LLMs to provide training or practice. There are user interfaces for LLMs which include voice interfaces so that your speaking can be transcribed (such as through using OpenAI's Whisper API). No doubt we will see more lawyer specific training programs in the near future using this technology. Some of the many potential types of training may include:

➢ Case Simulations: LLMs can simulate different case scenarios, allowing lawyers to practice their arguments or strategies.

➢ Legal Research Training: LLMs can be used to teach lawyers how to conduct effective legal research, providing tips and strategies.

➢ Client Communication Practice: LLMs can simulate client conversations, helping lawyers to practice their communication skills.

➢ Cross-Examination Practice: LLMs can simulate a witness or opposing counsel for cross-examination practice.

➢ Mock Negotiations: LLMs can simulate negotiations, providing lawyers with a safe environment to practice their negotiation skills.

➢ Language Skill Improvement: LLMs can assist lawyers in improving their legal writing and speaking skills.

➢ Cultural Sensitivity Training: LLMs can simulate interactions with clients from diverse cultural backgrounds, helping lawyers to develop cultural sensitivity.

➢ Preparation for Court Appearances: LLMs can simulate a courtroom scenario to help lawyers practice for real court appearances.

> ➤ Legal Tech Familiarization: LLMs can help lawyers become more comfortable with using technology in their practice.

> ➤ Stress Management: LLMs can help lawyers learn and practice stress management techniques.

Of course, do not be limited to these types of training or simulations. A motivated lawyer, assisted with their LLM has an amazing opportunity to learn, practice, and better themselves.

# CHAPTER EIGHT

## Workflows

When using LLMs, although being able to receive answers to questions can be helpful and interesting, it is especially powerful once you put this tool in the context of workflows and processes. When you design a workflow, you are breaking a problem or task into smaller or manageable tasks and considering the dependencies between tasks. For example, the output from one task may be needed as the input to another task.

There are likely many opportunities in your current practice to adjust and refine workflows so that certain tasks in a workflow may be performed by a LLM or by machine automation to result in a better performing or more efficient processes. This may include tasks which you are performing yourself or tasks which you have delegated to others who are performing on your behalf.

When integrating LLM usage into your workflow, you will need to identify what outputs you want from the LLM, and which inputs are required in order to obtain those outputs. Thus, this requires determining how to formulate your prompts to obtain the results you desire.

There are various tools which you can use today to help you automate workflows without requiring programming. These includes tools such as Microsoft Power Automate, Zapier, PabblyConnect, and many others. As LLM functionality begins to be incorporated into leading applications, creating workflows will continue to become easier and there will be more opportunities for improved efficiencies.

## *Prompt chaining*

In some instances a workflow may be a collection of prompts. Prompt chaining is one way to describe where an output from one prompt is used as input to another prompt. In your workflows you might have multiple steps which are performed sequentially by an LLM. Keep in mind that if using multiple prompts within the same chat, subject to limitations on the size of the context window, prior prompts and responses will be used to provide output. Many times this will be helpful as additional context is desirable. However, there may be times where you want to consider starting a new chat.

## *Human interjection*

Your process might need to decompose a larger task into smaller separate tasks in part so that you can inject human review or approval at different points in the process in order to obtain the desired result and make changes to help move the process forward in the desired direction. Similar to when you are collaborating with a person, if you do not check in frequently enough, the direction the process goes might begin to drift further and further from what you intend.

For example, suppose you are drafting a reply brief. How might you generate a workflow which uses an LLM but also other tools, including your intellect and expert legal judgment, to generate quality work product in the best manner?

You might begin by considering how you approach this type of work. Perhaps you might first represent the process as:

> ➤ Read and understand the respondent's brief.

> ➤ Identify key points of contention.

> ➤ Conduct legal research.

> ➤ Verify facts.

> ➤ Draft reply brief.

➢ Check citations.

➢ Proofread and edit.

➢ Review by senior attorney.

➢ Finalize and File.

Some of these tasks may be readily delegated to others in your current workflow. However, even among these tasks, there are many potential sub-tasks that might be present.

For example, the first task is to read and understand the respondent's brief. How might this task be broken up in a way that LLMs can help you to do that? Some potential sub-tasks which might be performed by an LLM include:

➢ Summarize the respondent's brief.

➢ Extract all citations to legal authorities from respondent's brief.

➢ Summarize each of the cases cited in respondent's brief.

➢ Identify each factual representation made in respondent's brief.

➢ Identify each argument made in respondent's brief.

➢ For each argument, identify any errors in logic in the argument.

If you had a report with this information, would it help you in terms of crystallizing your thinking earlier on? For most of us, this would be immensely helpful, but not all of these subtasks are necessarily a part of our current workflow. When relying on ourselves or other humans to perform this work, it simply may not have been considered cost effective or taking such steps would take more time than available. Yet, these issues are avoided when using an LLM.

Thus there are good reasons that we might treat workflows differently when steps are performed by humans instead of machines. Perhaps the steps take too long if performed by humans. The steps may need to be performed differently. So creating a workflow using LLMs is different than the way we might create a workflow where tasks are being performed by humans. Workflows should be constructed in a manner which takes into consideration both the strengths and weaknesses of LLMs and humans.

But take a moment and consider the possibilities of having the right information presented in the right way to help you perform an analysis or perform a writing task. Imagine how much faster and better you can do your work when you have such tools available.

Of course, many software developers are out there right now, trying to understand different legal tasks and how to automate them in a way that incorporates LLMs. Some tools exist today, and it will quickly become increasingly easier for you to automate your own workflows without programming using appropriate prompts to an

LLMs and collecting appropriate inputs and obtaining desired outputs.

If you are exploring your workflows and need help, you can consider using a prompt such as the following.

> You are my expert in workflow automation and process improvement for my law firm. Your goal is to help me create the best possible workflows for my needs. This includes generating the best possible prompts for my needs and making recommendations as to how different processes should be divided into different tasks and which tasks can be best performed by ChatGPT and what human input is needed at what points in the process. Tasks may be performed by an attorney, a staff member, or ChatGPT. My office uses Microsoft Office, including Microsoft Word, Microsoft PowerPoint, Microsoft Outlook, and Microsoft Excel. Your first response will be to ask me about a particular process or workflow which I want to improve. You will then ask me 3 questions regarding additional information about the process or workflow you may need in order to better understand the process. After that you will generate 3 different example workflows which optimize and improve the process in order to deliver higher quality results, faster results.

The above example is a specific prompt which is structured to help collect additional context regarding a workflow. When working with an LLM, keep in mind that you can break a process down into multiple back and forth exchanges like this to help provide more context and increase the likelihood of obtaining useful results.

## *Example workflow: form letter with form fields*

There have already been some example workflows or partial workflows presented. For example, creating a Microsoft PowerPoint presentation involved both an LLM and Microsoft PowerPoint and the output from the LLM was structured in a manner to facilitate its use in Microsoft PowerPoint.

One of the key takeaways I want you to have from this book, is do not just think about ChatGPT or other LLMs as applications, think of it as tools in a workflow and how it can be used to serve multiple purposes within a workflow or serve multiple functions within a workflow. Then think about how to automate processes or how to make the most of a collaboration with the LLM.

Think about what type of input is needed (i.e. the prompt) in order to start the workflow and then what additional input might be used along the way (human injection points) in order to consistently obtain useful results. There may be vast opportunities to improve efficiency for you and your staff.

One earlier example is to draft form letters. If you are using a docketing system that inserts form fields of a particular type in the form letters, then why not have the LLM include the appropriate form fields in the form letter being drafted?

Please write a form letter reporting that a client's U.S. patent has been issued and informing them of its issue date, when maintenance fees are due, when the patent will expire, and advising them of the benefits of patent marking. The form letter should use relevant fields from the following list of fields in the docketing software.

General Now     {General.Now}

General CurrentUser     {General.CurrentUser}

General EmailPostamble       {General.EmailPostamble}

Matter  AbandonedDate{Matter.AbandonedDate}

Matter  Abstract       {Matter.Abstract}

Matter  ActualCost     {Matter.ActualCost}

Matter  AdverseParties {Matter.AdverseParties}

Matter  AdverseParty<n>       {Matter.AdverseParty<n>}

Matter  Applicants     {Matter.Applicants}

Matter  Applicant<n>   {Matter.Applicant<n>}

Matter  AllowanceDate  {Matter.AllowanceDate}

Matter  Application       or       Serial       Number {Matter.ApplicationNum}

Matter  ArtUnit {Matter.ArtUnit}

Matter  Assignees      {Matter.Assignees}

Matter  Assignee<n>    {Matter.Assignee<n>}    [remaining form fields omitted]

Note that additional form fields were omitted.

Dear {Contact.First} {Contact.Last},

Subject: Issuance of U.S. Patent - {Matter.Title}

I am writing to inform you that your U.S. Patent, bearing the title "{Matter.Title}", has been officially issued by the United States Patent and Trademark Office (USPTO).

The details of your issued patent are as follows:

- Patent Number: {Matter.PatentNum}

- Issue Date: {Matter.IssueDate}

- Inventor(s): {Matter.InventorsEtAl}

- Assignee: {Matter.Assignees}

The patent claims can be summarized as "{Matter.Abstract}", and the full patent can be accessed on the USPTO website using the patent number provided above. Please review the issued patent to confirm that all information is correct.

The lifespan of a U.S. patent is generally 20 years from the filing date, meaning your patent is expected to expire on {Matter.ExpiredDate}.

Maintenance fees are necessary to keep your patent in force for its full term. These fees are due at 3.5, 7.5, and 11.5 years from the issue date. Please mark your calendar for these important dates:

- First Maintenance Fee Due: {Matter.IssueDate + 3.5 years}

- Second Maintenance Fee Due: {Matter.IssueDate + 7.5 years}

- Third Maintenance Fee Due: {Matter.IssueDate + 11.5 years}

---

I would also like to take this opportunity to remind you of the benefits of proper patent marking. Marking your product with the patent number alerts the public to the existence of your patent and can potentially increase the damages you can collect in the event of infringement.

Please feel free to contact me if you need further information or clarification regarding your issued patent, the maintenance fee schedule, or patent marking.

Thank you for choosing {Matter.LawFirm} as your partner in this process. We look forward to serving you in the future.

Best regards,

{General.CurrentUser}    {Contact.Title}    {Contact.Phone} {Contact.Email} {General.EmailPostamble}

---

In the above example, form fields were added in appropriate places in appropriate formats. By having an appropriate prompt, the output will need less modification before it can be used by the docketing software.

Suppose an attorney typically drafts form letters, then perhaps it is reviewed by others. Then an assistant enters the form letter into the docketing system adding appropriate fields.

Adding form fields manually can be one of the most tedious and unpleasant as well as time-consuming, so considerable time can be saved for the assistant, by thinking through how the output is going to be ultimately used and generating an appropriate prompt strategy to not just save the attorney time but also the assistant. Now multiplying that by every new form letter or every review and revision to existing form letters and a little bit of extra effort in formulating a prompt that better fits the workflow provides significant benefit!

# GOODHUE

# CHAPTER NINE

# Law practice management

There are numerous opportunities for using LLMs in the management aspects of your law firm today. Not all of these are lawyering tasks. LLMs can be particularly good at drafting documents which might be relevant to management.

## *Job descriptions*

With extraordinarily little information, an LLM like ChatGPT can draft a job description for a particular position. The more detailed information provided the more specific the job description which is generated. However, even with a general prompt a job description which may be edited can be created and the LLM may identify one or more items to include which you agree with, but you may not have thought to include.

Please write a job description for a paralegal for a law firm which is focused on wills and trusts.

Company: [Law Firm Name]

Location: [City, State]

About Us: [Law Firm Name] is a well-established and respected law firm that specializes in wills, trusts, and estate planning. Our mission is to provide exceptional legal services and personalized solutions for our clients in all aspects of estate planning and wealth preservation. We are seeking a dedicated and detail-oriented paralegal to join our growing team and support our attorneys in providing excellent client service.

Job Summary: The Paralegal - Wills and Trusts will play a crucial role in our firm's wills and trusts practice area by assisting our attorneys in drafting and reviewing legal documents, conducting legal research, and managing client files. The successful candidate will have a solid understanding of the principles of wills, trusts, and estate planning, along with excellent communication and organizational skills.

Responsibilities:

1.      Assist attorneys in drafting, revising, and finalizing wills, trusts, and other estate planning documents.

2.      Conduct thorough legal research on various matters related to wills, trusts, and estate planning.

3.      Manage and maintain client files, ensuring all documents are up-to-date and organized.

4.      Communicate effectively with clients, attorneys, and other team members in a professional and timely manner.

5.      Obtain, review, and organize relevant documents and information from clients and third parties.

6.      Assist with the preparation and filing of probate court documents.

7.      Prepare and maintain detailed indexes of estate planning documents and client correspondence.

8.      Monitor and track deadlines for various tasks and ensure they are completed in a timely manner.

9.      Stay current on changes in laws and regulations pertaining to wills, trusts, and estate planning.

10.     Perform other duties as assigned by attorneys and management.

Qualifications:

1.      Paralegal certification or an associate degree in paralegal studies from an accredited program.

2.      At least 2 years of experience as a paralegal, preferably in a law firm specializing in wills and trusts.

3.      Strong knowledge of legal principles related to wills, trusts, and estate planning.

4.      Excellent written and verbal communication skills, with a keen attention to detail.

5.      Proficiency in Microsoft Office applications (Word, Excel, Outlook) and legal research platforms (e.g., Westlaw, LexisNexis).

---

6.      Strong organizational and time-management skills, with the ability to prioritize tasks and work under pressure.

7.      Professional demeanor and commitment to maintaining client confidentiality.

8.      Ability to work independently and collaboratively within a team environment.

[Law Firm Name] offers a competitive salary and benefits package, including health insurance, retirement plan, and paid time off. We are an equal opportunity employer and welcome candidates from diverse backgrounds to apply.

To apply, please submit your resume, cover letter, and salary requirements to [email address]. We look forward to reviewing your application.

---

There are potential issues with the above job description. For example in some jurisdictions, the salary range may need to be included and include no salary posted or there may be other legal concerns. In addition, it may be that the qualification list is so detailed and specific that there may not be sufficiently qualified applicants in a particular market. Thus, like all LLM generated content, one should review and give critical thought to the approach taken. However, this is an area where LLMs often shine in terms of generating content which one does not routinely generate on their own and so being able to generate a reasonable first draft can provide a significant productivity boost.

## *Policies and procedures*

Another area of law firm management where LLMs can be immensely helpful is drafting policies and procedures such as for use in training that new hire. Training can be expedited where there is a comprehensive and up-to-date training manual, but creating and maintaining such documentation can introduce significant overhead, especially for a smaller organization.

An LLM can be helpful in that it can decompose a seemingly simple task into a number of different sub-tasks, so that it is incredibly clear to an employee how to perform the task. Even with little input an LLM can generate a reasonable procedure.

Please generate a law firm procedure for processing checks received in the mail.ease write a job description for a paralegal for a law firm which is focused on wills and trusts.

Law Firm Procedure for Processing Checks Received in the Mail

Purpose: This procedure outlines the steps to be followed when processing checks received in the mail at [Law Firm Name]. Adherence to this procedure ensures that checks are processed promptly, accurately, and securely, reducing the risk of lost or misplaced funds.

Scope: This procedure applies to all employees of [Law Firm Name] who are responsible for handling and processing checks received in the mail, including administrative staff, paralegals, and attorneys.

123

Procedure:

1.      Check Retrieval and Initial Handling a. Collect incoming mail from the designated mail area. b. Sort through the mail, identifying and separating all envelopes containing checks. c. Clearly mark each envelope containing a check with a "Check Enclosed" stamp or a similar indicator.

2.      Opening and Recording a. Open envelopes containing checks using a letter opener, taking care not to damage the enclosed check. b. Review the check for accuracy, ensuring the following information is correct:

•       Payee: [Law Firm Name]

•       Date

•       Amount

•       Signature c. Record the details of the check in the firm's check log, including:

•       Date received

•       Payer's name

•       Check number

•       Check amount

•       Client/matter number (if applicable)

•       Purpose (e.g., retainer, invoice payment, settlement) d. Make a photocopy of the check and attach it to a copy of the corresponding invoice or receipt (if applicable).

3.      Endorsement and Secure Storage a. Endorse the check with the firm's bank account information and a "For Deposit Only" stamp. b. Securely store the check in a locked drawer or safe designated for holding checks until deposit.

c. Update the client's account or billing records to reflect the received payment.

4. Deposit Preparation and Record-Keeping a. Assemble all checks to be deposited along with the necessary deposit slips. b. Complete the deposit slip, listing each check separately and calculating the total deposit amount. c. Verify that the deposit slip total matches the sum of the checks being deposited. d. Make a copy of the completed deposit slip for the firm's records.

5. Check Deposit a. Transport the checks and deposit slip to the bank for deposit. Ensure that checks are securely stored during transport. b. Obtain a deposit receipt from the bank and verify the deposit amount for accuracy. c. Attach the deposit receipt to the copy of the deposit slip and file it in the firm's financial records.

6. Reconciliation and Follow-Up a. Reconcile the deposited checks with the firm's financial records, including bank statements, on a monthly basis. b. Follow up on any discrepancies or issues with the bank or the payer, as necessary.

7. Confidentiality and Security a. Maintain strict confidentiality when handling checks and client information. b. Dispose of all check-related materials securely (e.g., using a cross-cut shredder) once they are no longer needed, following the firm's document retention policy.

In reviewing the output, this might not match your procedure. For example, you may need explanation on determining what account checks should be deposited to and separate operating accounts from trust accounts. So either a different prompt may be needed, or the generated output would need to be revised. In addition, perhaps you need to set different starting points and end points to the process as perhaps some of the procedure is performed by an assistant and other parts of the procedure are performed by a bookkeeper. However, as with the job description listing, the output is likely to include information or steps which may not have occurred to you to include.

Thus, any number of other policies may be drafted whether it is a parental leave policy, a collections policy (including sample emails or letters to be sent to clients with overdue bills), or anything else. One could even use an LLM to generate policies regarding the use of LLMs.

 Please draft a policy for law firm use of LLMs such as ChatGPT. The policy should take into consideration ethics of using LLMs including client confidentiality, potential bias in LLMs, the possibility for inaccurate information and not relying on LLMs for legal conclusions.

 Policy Title: Use of Language Model (LLM) Technologies in Legal Practice

Effective Date: [Date]

Policy Statement: [Law Firm Name] recognizes the potential benefits of using LLM technologies, such as ChatGPT, in legal practice to enhance efficiency and productivity. However, the firm is also aware of the ethical considerations and potential risks associated with the use of these technologies. This policy outlines the guidelines for using LLMs responsibly, ensuring compliance with legal and ethical obligations, including client confidentiality, potential bias, accuracy of information, and avoiding reliance on LLMs for legal conclusions.

Scope: This policy applies to all employees of [Law Firm Name] who utilize LLM technologies in their work.

Guidelines:

1. Client Confidentiality a. Employees must ensure that they do not disclose any confidential client information when using LLMs, including names, case details, or any other identifiable information. b. When seeking assistance from an LLM, use hypothetical situations and anonymized data to preserve client confidentiality.

2. Potential Bias a. Employees must be aware of potential biases that may be present in LLM outputs, as these models have been trained on vast amounts of data from various sources and may inadvertently reflect societal biases. b. Exercise critical thinking and professional judgment when reviewing LLM-generated content to identify and address any potential biases or issues.

3. Accuracy of Information a. LLMs may provide information that is outdated, incomplete, or inaccurate. It is the responsibility of the employee to verify the accuracy of LLM-generated content by conducting independent research and consulting reliable sources, such as legal databases, statutes, and case law. b. If any inaccuracies or inconsistencies are identified in LLM-generated content, employees should disregard the information and not use it in their work.

4. Legal Conclusions a. Employees must not rely solely on LLMs for legal conclusions or advice. While LLMs can provide general guidance and support, they cannot replace the professional judgment and expertise of an attorney. b. LLM-generated content should be used as a starting point for research and analysis. Employees must independently evaluate the applicability and relevance of the information to their specific case and circumstances.

5. Supervision and Training a. Employees must receive appropriate training on the responsible use of LLM technologies in legal practice, including ethical considerations and potential risks. b. The use of LLMs should be supervised by an attorney or a designated

employee who is knowledgeable about the technology and its limitations.

6. Disclosure to Clients a. When LLM-generated content is used as part of a work product provided to a client, the client should be informed about the role of the LLM in generating the content. b. Clients should be assured that LLM-generated content has been reviewed and approved by an attorney before it is shared with them.

7. Monitoring and Review a. [Law Firm Name] will periodically review the use of LLM technologies to ensure compliance with this policy and assess any potential risks or issues that may arise. b. Employees are encouraged to provide feedback on their experiences with LLMs to help improve the firm's understanding and responsible use of these technologies.

By adhering to this policy, [Law Firm Name] seeks to maintain the highest ethical standards in the use of LLM technologies while leveraging their potential to improve our legal services. Employees must familiarize themselves with this policy and ensure compliance in their use of LLMs.

You should also keep in mind that you no doubt have clients that are using LLMs for their own policies and procedures related to their business.

## *Training*

Following are two sets of attorney billing entries which intentionally do not identify company names or individuals. The first set is an example of higher quality billing entries. The second set are billing entries which may need rewritten and improved. Please review and revise the billing entires in the second set and provide suggestions in order to make these billing entries more understandable to clients, more accurate, and convey value received. Care should be taken not to overstate the activity performed, not to overstate the thoroughness of the activity performed, to avoid creating any expectations regarding outcomes, or to characterize in a manner which may differ from the client's characterization. Exemplary set [exemplary billing entries omitted]. Set to improve [billing entries to improve omitted].

Perhaps, you have attorneys or other timekeepers that need to improve their billing entry practices. Having the timekeepers run their billing entries through a LLM before submitting may help them learn and decrease the amount of time a billing attorney needs to spend. Of course, this is one of those instances, where you would want to choose an LLM with practices which would not violate obligations regarding confidentiality, or else, as in the example, remove all identifying information from the prompt.

## Spreadsheets

If working with spreadsheets, there are several ways that LLMs can help. When you are creating prompts to generate spreadsheets, more specificity, precision, and overall context is often required to obtain the results you want. However, it is possible to generate the information needed to cut and paste into a spreadsheet program like Microsoft Excel. The following is an example of such a prompt.

Prepare a spreadsheet template for a litigation budget, thinking step-by-step. The budget should include have categories for (1) case assessment, development and administration, (2) pre-trial pleadings and motions, (3) discovery, and (4) trial preparation and trial. Each of these categories should be further divided into relevant sub-categories which you will generate with formulas for totals for each sub-category, totals for each category, and overall total. For each sub-category there should be an estimate for shareholder hours, shareholder rate, associate hours, associate rate, and paralegal hours and paralegal rate and formulas to determine dollar totals for each person. The budget should also include at the bottom prominent notice that this is an estimate only. Use a 0.0 for any hours, use $500 for the shareholder rate and $300 for the associate rate, and $100 for the paralegal rate. The output should be provided as text suitable for cutting and pasting into Microsoft Excel beginning at column A, row 1 and tabs should be used to separate data in columns and new paragraphs for separating the end of a row and the beginning of the next. Please provide only the text for the spreadsheet suitable for cutting and pasting (i.e. do not place items in quotation marks), no other explanation, no comments. Provide the output in a code window.

The above prompt is extremely specific as to what is requested and is the result of several iterations. Some of the context communicated includes:

➢ Explaining that the output is for cutting and pasting into Microsoft Excel.

➢ Specifying the location A1, where the output will be cut and pasted in Microsoft Excel

➢ Specifying that tabs should separate data between columns and new paragraphs should be used to separate rows.

➢ Suppressing extraneous explanation and comments.

➢ Providing the output in a code window (to make it easier to cut and paste).

The result is text within a code window:

```plaintext                                                    Copy code

Category    Sub-Category    Shareholder Hours    Shareholder Rate ($)    Asso

Case Assessment, Development and Administration Case Assessment 0.0 500 0.0
Case Assessment, Development and Administration Development 0.0 500 0.0 300
Case Assessment, Development and Administration Administration  0.0 500 0.0
Case Assessment, Development and Administration Total    = SUM(C2:C4)

Pre-trial Pleadings and Motions Initial Pleadings   0.0 500 0.0 300 0.0 100
Pre-trial Pleadings and Motions Responses   0.0 500 0.0 300 0.0 100 = C8*D8
Pre-trial Pleadings and Motions Motions 0.0 500 0.0 300 0.0 100 = C9*D9 = E9
Pre-trial Pleadings and Motions Total    = SUM(C7:C9)       = SUM(E7:E9)

Discovery    Document Review 0.0 500 0.0 300 0.0 100 = C12*D12    = E12*F12
Discovery    Depositions 0.0 500 0.0 300 0.0 100 = C13*D13    = E13*F13    = H1
Discovery    Interrogatories 0.0 500 0.0 300 0.0 100 = C14*D14    = E14*F14
Discovery    Total    = SUM(C12:C14)       = SUM(E12:E14)       = SUM(H12:H14)
```

This text can then be cut and pasted into Microsoft Excel at column A, row 1 (cell: A1). Once this is complete, the spreadsheet looks like the following screenshot.

| | A | B | C | D | E | F | G | H | I | J | K | L | M |
|---|---|---|---|---|---|---|---|---|---|---|---|---|---|
| 1 | Category | Sub-Category | Shareholder Hou | Shareholc | Associate | Associate | Paralegal | Paralegal | Shareholc | Associate | Paralegal | Sub-Category Total (S |
| 2 | | | | | | | | | | | | |
| 3 | Case Assessment, Develoj | Case Assessment | 0 | 500 | 0 | 300 | 0 | 100 | 0 | 0 | 0 | 0 |
| 4 | Case Assessment, Deve | Development | 0 | 500 | 0 | 300 | 0 | 100 | 0 | 0 | 0 | 0 |
| 5 | Case Assessment, Develoj | Administration | 0 | 500 | 0 | 300 | 0 | 100 | 0 | 0 | 0 | 0 |
| 6 | Case Assessment, Deve | Total | 0 | | 0 | | 0 | | 0 | 0 | 0 | 0 |
| 7 | | | | | | | | | | | | |
| 8 | Pre-trial Pleadings and | Initial Pleadings | 0 | 500 | 0 | 300 | 0 | 100 | 0 | 0 | 0 | 0 |
| 9 | Pre-trial Pleadings and M | Responses | 0 | 500 | 0 | 300 | 0 | 100 | 0 | 0 | 0 | 0 |
| 10 | Pre-trial Pleadings and | Motions | 0 | 500 | 0 | 300 | 0 | 100 | 0 | 0 | 0 | 0 |
| 11 | Pre-trial Pleadings and | Total | 0 | | 0 | | 0 | | 0 | 0 | 0 | 0 |
| 12 | | | | | | | | | | | | |
| 13 | Discovery | Document Review | 0 | 500 | 0 | 300 | 0 | 100 | 0 | 0 | 0 | 0 |
| 14 | Discovery | Depositions | 0 | 500 | 0 | 300 | 0 | 100 | 0 | 0 | 0 | 0 |
| 15 | Discovery | Interrogatories | 0 | 500 | 0 | 300 | 0 | 100 | 0 | 0 | 0 | 0 |
| 16 | Discovery | Total | 0 | | 0 | | 0 | | 0 | 0 | 0 | 0 |
| 17 | Trial Preparation and Trial | Pre-Trial Motions | 0 | 500 | 0 | 300 | 0 | 100 | 0 | 0 | 0 | 0 |
| 18 | Trial Preparation and Trial | Witness Preparation | 0 | 500 | 0 | 300 | 0 | 100 | 0 | 0 | 0 | 0 |
| 19 | Trial Preparation and Trial | Trial | 0 | 500 | 0 | 300 | 0 | 100 | 0 | 0 | 0 | 0 |
| 20 | Trial Preparation and Trial | Total | 0 | | 0 | | 0 | | 0 | 0 | 0 | 0 |
| 21 | | | | | | | | | | | | |
| 22 | Total | | 0 | | 0 | | 300 | | 0 | 0 | 0 | 0 |

## *Graphs and Charts*

Even where an LLM cannot independently generate a desired graph or chart on its own, it can still help you do so.

Generate a bar graph for an associate attorney's hours for 2022. The monthly total of hours from January to December are 145, 124, 151, 111, 146, 164,130,150, 144,145,142,157.

As an AI language model, I'm unable to create visual graphics directly. However, I can help you with the data and guide you on how to create a bar graph using a tool like Microsoft Excel, Google Sheets, or any other data visualization tool.

Here's the data you provided:

Month   Hours

January145

February 124

March 151

April 111

May 146

June 164

July 130

August 150

September 144

October 145

November 142

December 157

To create a bar graph using Microsoft Excel or Google Sheets, follow these steps:

1.      Open a new spreadsheet in Microsoft Excel or Google Sheets.

2.      Copy and paste the data above into the spreadsheet.

3.      Select the entire data range (including the headers).

4.      In Excel, go to the 'Insert' tab and click on 'Column or Bar Chart.' In Google Sheets, go to 'Insert' and click on 'Chart.'

5.      Choose the 'Bar' or 'Column' chart type.

6.      Customize the chart by adding a title, axis labels, and formatting as desired.

After following these steps, you should have a bar graph representing the associate attorney's monthly hours for 2022.

---

Although this output may be sufficiently helpful, despite the LLM's stated limitations, there are more efficient ways to indirectly create the desired graph.

Generate code for a Microsoft Excel macro to create the bar graph with the data provided.

Here's a VBA macro code you can use to create a bar graph in Microsoft Excel based on the data provided:

```vba
Sub CreateBarGraph()

    Dim ws As Worksheet
    Dim chart As Chart

    ' Create a new worksheet to hold the data
    Set ws = ThisWorkbook.Worksheets.Add
    ws.Name = "AssociateHours"

    ' Enter the data
    ws.Cells(1, 1).Value = "Month"
    ws.Cells(1, 2).Value = "Hours"
    ws.Cells(2, 1).Value = "January"
    ws.Cells(2, 2).Value = 145
    ws.Cells(3, 1).Value = "February"
    ws.Cells(3, 2).Value = 124
    ws.Cells(4, 1).Value = "March"
    ws.Cells(4, 2).Value = 151
    ws.Cells(5, 1).Value = "April"
    ws.Cells(5, 2).Value = 111
    ws.Cells(6, 1).Value = "May"
    ws.Cells(6, 2).Value = 146
    ws.Cells(7, 1).Value =
```

⟳ Regenerate response

To use this macro, follow these steps:

1. Open Microsoft Excel and press ALT + F11 to open the Visual Basic for Applications (VBA) editor.

2. Go to Insert > Module to insert a new module.

3. Copy and paste the VBA code provided above into the module.

4. Press CTRL + S to save the workbook. Make sure to save it as an Excel Macro-Enabled Workbook (*.xlsm) to preserve the macro.

5. Press ALT + Q to close the VBA editor and return to the Excel workbook.

6. Press ALT + F8 to open the Macro dialog box.

7. Select the macro named CreateBarGraph and click Run.

After running the macro, a new worksheet will be created with the provided data, and a bar graph will be generated based on that data.

We can then follow the steps provided and we will have a Microsoft Excel worksheet with the data provided and the requested bar graph.

Although the ability to create code including macros can be an enormously powerful tool and does not require understanding the code, it may be an iterative approach and you may need to ask the LLM to debug, revise, or edit the code if it does not provide the desired output. Generally this can be performed by simply stating in your prompt what result you obtained, what result you wanted, and asking the LLM to modify the code to provide the result desired.

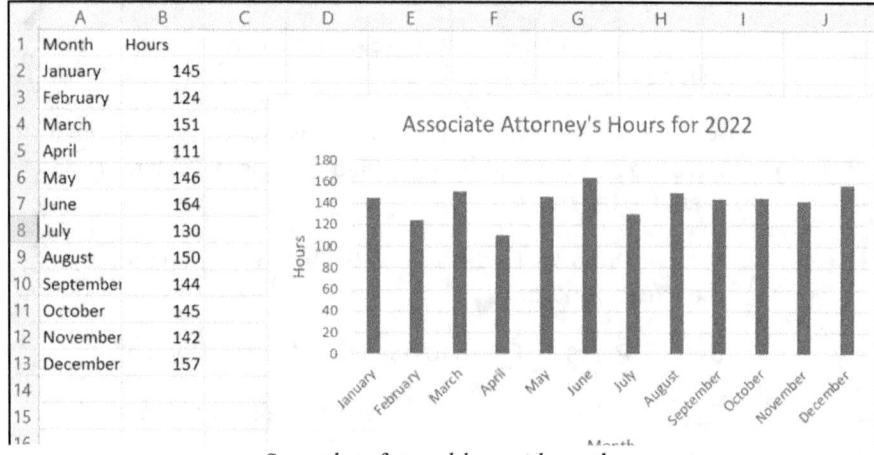

| | A | B |
|---|---|---|
| 1 | Month | Hours |
| 2 | January | 145 |
| 3 | February | 124 |
| 4 | March | 151 |
| 5 | April | 111 |
| 6 | May | 146 |
| 7 | June | 164 |
| 8 | July | 130 |
| 9 | August | 150 |
| 10 | September | 144 |
| 11 | October | 145 |
| 12 | November | 142 |
| 13 | December | 157 |
| 14 | | |
| 15 | | |
| 16 | | |

*Screenshot of spreadsheet with graph.*

# CHAPTER TEN

## Lawyer marketing

Another one of the easiest and perhaps best areas to apply LLMs is when performing internal tasks such as lawyer marketing. This might include:

➤ Preparing articles for newsletters

➤ Generating blog posts

➤ Generating content for your web site

➤ Creating social media posts

> ➤ Scripts for video

A growing number of individuals and businesses are using LLM generated content on their web sites, social media, and elsewhere. One of the legitimate concerns is that there will be a content explosion of machine-generated content which ultimately will not be of value to users when they can use an LLM to generate their own content.

This does not mean you should not use LLMs for these tasks, but you should be strategic in your use of LLMs. For example, select topics which are more particular to you and personalize the content generated so that it is in your voice and your style, and is otherwise original to you. Include your own experiences or stories. This may also mean being more creative with your prompts to help achieve these goals.

## Generate articles / posts

A common use of LLMs is to generate articles or posts. Suppose we are an employment lawyer and have decided it would be a promising idea to remind our clients not to rely on LLMs to generate policies or procedure, at least not without legal review.

You are a lawyer drafting a post for marketing purposes. The post should include 5 reasons along with specific hypothetical examples where reliance on an LLM results in increased risk. All the examples should relate to employment law with the intention of making sure readers know that it is a mistake to rely on an LLM to generate HR policies or procedures without at least attorney review.

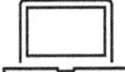

As advances in artificial intelligence continue to transform various industries, we are starting to see large language models (LLMs) being used in an increasingly wide array of applications. However, while LLMs have their advantages, they should not be used as a standalone solution for generating HR policies or procedures. Here are five reasons, along with specific hypothetical examples, illustrating why reliance on an LLM can result in increased risk, particularly in the field of employment law:

1. Lack of Contextual Understanding: LLMs can't fully grasp the nuances of specific workplace environments or the unique circumstances of individual employees. For example, an LLM might suggest a generic policy on flexible work hours, but it wouldn't account for specific roles or departments that require staff presence during certain hours. This could lead to a poorly tailored policy that disrupts business operations.

2. Absence of Legal Judgment: LLMs are not capable of legal reasoning or judgment. They can't evaluate the potential risks or ramifications of certain policies. If an LLM generates a policy regarding social media use that inadvertently infringes upon an employee's right to engage in protected concerted activities under the National Labor Relations Act, the company could face legal repercussions.

3. Inability to Stay Current with Changing Laws: Employment laws and regulations frequently change, and LLMs, especially those not regularly updated, may not reflect these changes. For instance, if an LLM generates a policy on employee leaves based on outdated Family and Medical Leave Act regulations, it could expose the company to unnecessary legal risk.

4. No Ethical or Moral Reasoning: LLMs cannot understand or apply ethical or moral reasoning, a critical component of many HR decisions. For example, an LLM might suggest a policy that technically complies with anti-discrimination laws but fails to promote a diverse and

inclusive workplace culture. This could lead to employee dissatisfaction and harm the company's reputation.

5.      Risk of Misinterpretation: LLMs can be prone to errors or misinterpretations. For instance, an LLM might generate an overly strict or ambiguous harassment policy, leading to confusion among employees and potentially creating a hostile work environment.

In conclusion, while LLMs can serve as a helpful tool, they should not be the sole source for generating HR policies or procedures. Engaging an attorney to review and guide these processes is essential to ensuring legal compliance and mitigating risk. Always remember, when it comes to your company and your employees, it's better to be safe than sorry!

---

The results are reasonable, but in this instance, the article or post seems a little artificial and formal. Perhaps you can expand upon the examples or interject your personal experiences. In addition, this does not appear to be in your style. You can make it more in your style just by having an example of something you have written and providing the appropriate instructions.

Although I am not an employment lawyer and so do not have writings about the subject to use as an example, I instead used an introduction to a book for corporate inventors.

 Please rewrite the above article in a tone and stye more consistent with me. To determine my tone and style, please review the following example of my writing: [writing sample omitted].

Artificial intelligence is taking strides by the day, and large language models (LLMs) are finding their way into a broad spectrum of applications. However, as fascinating as they are, it's crucial to remember that LLMs aren't the silver bullet for all your HR policy and procedure needs. Here are five reasons, each with a hypothetical situation, to illustrate why depending solely on an LLM in the realm of employment law could be akin to skating on thin ice:

1.     Short on Context: LLMs may be intelligent, but they don't quite understand the unique dynamics of your workplace or the individual stories of your employees. Suppose an LLM recommends a one-size-fits-all policy on flexible work hours, ignoring the specific needs of some roles or departments. This could lead to a not-so-great policy that throws a wrench in the smooth running of your business.

2.     Lacking Legal Wisdom: LLMs can't make legal judgments. They can't weigh the pros and cons of a policy from a legal standpoint. Imagine an LLM formulating a social media policy that unknowingly infringes upon an employee's rights under the National Labor Relations Act. That's a lawsuit waiting to happen!

3.     Not So Up-to-date: Employment laws change more frequently than the seasons, and an LLM, especially if not regularly updated, may not keep up. Picture an LLM creating a policy on employee leaves based on outdated Family and Medical Leave Act regulations. That's an invitation to unnecessary legal troubles.

4.     Lacks Ethical Compass: LLMs don't understand ethics or moral reasoning, an essential aspect of HR decisions. For instance, an LLM might suggest a policy that meets the bare minimum of anti-discrimination laws but fails to promote a workplace culture that celebrates diversity. This could lead to disgruntled employees and a tarnished company image.

5.     Mistakes Happen: LLMs can make errors or misinterpret information. Consider an LLM crafting a harassment policy that's too strict or vague, leading to confusion among employees and possibly creating an unfriendly work environment.

In short, while LLMs can be handy, they shouldn't be the be-all and end-all for creating HR policies or procedures. Having an attorney at the helm is the key to navigating legal compliance and dodging risk. Remember, it's always better to double-check than to risk a fall! As in our book "Dare To Invent," where we explore the complex but rewarding world of inventing and patenting, we understand that practical guidance, informed by professional expertise, is critical to success. The same applies here - consult your organization's legal counsel to tailor your HR policies to your unique needs. After all, the goal is not just to avoid legal pitfalls, but to create a thriving, supportive workplace for all.

A few principles are demonstrated in the above examples. First, detailed, and specific prompts can often provide better results. Second, examples are a powerful way to communicate what you want. Here, just providing an example of the desired tone and style made a significant difference in the output and less rewriting is required. Third, be willing to iterate. If you are not happy with the results, try again with a different prompt until you obtain what you want. Once you have figured out how to get a particular type of result, remember your prompt strategy for future use.

One way to save time and effort in your marketing is to re-purpose your content. An LLM can help you repurpose your content too!

Please rewrite the above into a series of tweets and add emojis throughout as appropriate

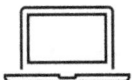

1.     AI is making strides, but Large Language Models (LLMs) aren't the magic solution for all HR needs! Here's why you shouldn't rely solely on an LLM for employment law. A thread...  #AI #EmploymentLaw

2.     Short on Context: LLMs don't get the unique dynamics of your workplace. They might suggest a one-size-fits-all policy that doesn't fit your business. Think roles that need specific work hours.  #AI #HR

3.     Lacking Legal Wisdom: LLMs can't make legal judgments. Imagine them creating a social media policy that infringes on employee rights - that's a lawsuit waiting to happen!  #AI #EmploymentLaw

4.     Not So Up-to-date: Employment laws change often. An LLM not updated regularly might base a leave policy on outdated laws. That's an invitation to legal troubles.

So if you have struggled to write tweets due to character number constraints, unfamiliarity with hash tags, or a limited emoji vocabulary, you now have the help you need.

## Generate content for web site

Thus, in addition to articles and posts, you can generate the type of content which might be useful to include on your web site. You can generate the copy for a complete web site very quickly and LLMs could even be used to generate the code!

If you are sure what type of content might be useful to include on a web site, you can ask.

I am planning a web site for a family law attorney. What are some examples of different types of content that should be included?

Creating a website for a family law attorney can be an exciting project. Here are some content ideas that you may consider:

1.      About Us: A section that talks about the attorney, their qualifications, years of experience, and unique value proposition. This section can also include professional photos, a personal statement, and any important recognitions or awards.

2.      Practice Areas: This section should detail the areas of family law that the attorney specializes in, such as divorce, child custody, child support, alimony, adoption, etc. Each of these practice areas could potentially have their own detailed page with more information.

3.      Case Studies/Success Stories: Showcasing previous successful cases can help potential clients understand the kind of work the attorney does and build trust. Make sure to maintain client confidentiality when sharing these stories.

4.      Blog/Articles: Regular blog posts or articles about relevant topics in family law can help demonstrate the attorney's expertise and keep the website fresh. This can also help with search engine optimization (SEO).

5.      Client Testimonials: Feedback from previous clients can help build trust and credibility.

6.      Frequently Asked Questions (FAQs): This section can address common questions that potential clients might have about family law processes, costs, timelines, etc.

7.      Contact Information: Clearly displayed contact information, including phone number, email, and physical

address if applicable, is crucial. You might also consider including a contact form for easy communication.

8.      Consultation Booking: An online system for booking initial consultations can make it easy for potential clients to get in touch.

9.      Resources: This could include links to relevant legal resources, downloadable forms or guides, and anything else that might be helpful for someone going through a family law issue.

10.     News & Updates: A section to post about recent developments in family law, updates to the firm, or community involvement.

11.     Legal Disclaimer: A necessary part of any legal website, this should include disclaimers about the advice given on the site, attorney-client relationships, etc.

12.     Multimedia Content: This could include video introductions, webinars, podcasts, or infographics to cater to different user preferences.

## *Frequently asked questions*

One of the ideas provided was to include FAQs. Many web sites have a list of questions. If you wish to include such a list, you can have an LLM generate a list of questions for you to review. This is an example of using an LLM to help generate ideas.

Please generate a list of 20 most commonly asked questions about patenting asked by businesses interested in protecting their products.

Sure, here are some commonly asked questions about patenting:

1.     What is a patent and why is it important for my business?

2.     How does a patent protect my product?

3.     What types of patents are there and which one is right for my product?

4.     How do I know if my product is patentable? [[remainder omitted].

Once you have identified ideas that you like, then you can have complete answers generated to your specifications.

Generate a one paragraph answer for each of question 1 and 2.

1.     What is a patent and why is it important for my business?

A patent is a form of intellectual property right granted by the government to an inventor. It gives the inventor the exclusive right to prevent others from making, using, selling, or importing the patented invention for a certain period of time, typically 20 years from the filing date. This exclusivity is important for businesses because it can provide a competitive advantage in the marketplace. By preventing others from copying your invention, a patent can help ensure that your business is the only one able to profit from the invention's use. Furthermore, patents can attract investment, add value to your business, and can be licensed or sold for additional revenue.

2. How does a patent protect my product?

A patent protects your product by giving you the legal authority to stop others from making, using, selling, or importing your patented invention without your permission. If someone infringes on your patent, you can take legal action against them to stop the infringement and potentially recover damages. This protection is enforced by the courts, and the specifics can vary depending on the jurisdiction. It's important to note that a patent doesn't give you the right to make or use your invention (as that could infringe on others' patents), but rather the right to exclude others from doing so. This is why conducting a thorough patent search and obtaining a freedom-to-operate opinion can be crucial steps in the patenting process.

FAQs are a good type of content to let an LLM help you with, as some of the questions generated may be so basic to you, that you would not have recognized them as questions which people have. In addition, the answers can be written in plain English and although you may need to modify, considerable time can be saved.

LLMs are also generally good at shorter form content like this. When generating longer content, sometimes there is too much drift as well as a lack of conciseness. This is also a reason you may have more success generating articles like in the examples where there are 5 items, or 10 items discussed.

## *Enhancing content*

If one already has a web site and one wants to optimize it, an LLM can help with that too.

# GOODHUE

Please review https://www.goodhue.com and provide specific small content changes or suggestions to improve search engine optimization or increase traffic with the least amount of effort. I do not want general advice, but a list of specific changes.

Based on my review of the Goodhue, Coleman & Owens, P.C. website, here are some specific content changes or suggestions that could help improve search engine optimization (SEO) or increase traffic:

Homepage: The homepage has a lot of valuable information about the services offered, but it lacks a clear meta description and keywords in the header. These are critical for search engines to understand the content of the page. For example, a potential meta description could be "Goodhue, Coleman & Owens, P.C. are experienced U.S. intellectual property lawyers helping businesses capture and build value using patents, trademarks, and copyrights."

Use of Keywords: While the website does mention important keywords such as "patents," "trademarks," "copyrights," and "intellectual property," these could be incorporated more frequently and naturally within the text to help improve SEO. Make sure the keyword density is in the 1-2% range for optimal SEO performance.

Client Testimonials: The testimonials on your site are great, but it would be beneficial to include the names or the industries of the clients who provided the testimonials. This could help with long-tail SEO and provide more credibility to the testimonials.

Blog/Publications: The website has a "Publications" tab, but it's unclear what kind of content this includes. If it's not already the case, consider publishing regular blog posts about relevant topics in intellectual property law. This will not only help with SEO but also demonstrate your expertise and keep visitors engaged.

Internal Linking: Make sure that all pages of the website are interconnected. This helps search engines crawl the site more effectively and can also help users navigate the site more easily.

Mobile Optimization: Ensure that the site is fully optimized for mobile users. This is important as more than half of all web traffic now comes from mobile devices.

Use of Images: Images can significantly enhance user engagement. Consider adding relevant images to your content, ensuring that each image has an alt text for SEO.

## Bios

There are various situations where you may be writing, speaking, or appearing on podcasts and you would like to tailor your bio to the particular publication or event and its audience and sometimes comport with word count limitations. You can use an LLM to review and rewrite your bio.

Please review my bio at https://www.goodhue.com/john.html and using the bio, draft an about the author for my upcoming book on large language models.

These are just some of the many ways that LLMs can help support your marketing efforts. If you have been meaning to increase your content marketing, then you really can save time and improve your work product by using LLMs to help you.

# CHAPTER ELEVEN

# Looking forward and conclusions

## *Looking forward*

The use of LLMs is rapidly evolving. Here is some of what you might see more of in the near future.

### *Widespread availability and use*

You will notice LLM features everywhere in every product. You are already seeing them in your search engines and there are integrations available with your Microsoft Office products. You are seeing them integrated into your legal research tools, case management software, and you will continue to see standalone offerings for specific tasks.

## *Use by non-lawyers*

Of course, you will see examples of agreements, demand letters, and other documents prepared by non-lawyers using LLM tools to provide documents that may superficially appear appropriate, but turn out to be ill-conceived. You may also find increased numbers of pro se filings made by pro se litigants using LLM tools to assist in their litigation.

There will be a growing number of services which help non-lawyers perform tasks which have generally been performed by lawyers.

## *Increased sophistication and customization*

Available tools will continue to increase in sophistication and will be customized to particular users or their applications. For example, in order to produce a better LLM for legal research, an LLM can be trained with higher quality practice materials, as well as legal research tools or an existing model may be fine-tuned to perform particular tasks. Some of the applications integrating LLMs take this approach to produce better outputs than ChatGPT.

Tools will allow you to train with your own data in order to provide results which better affect your practice or your law firm's practice.

You may work with corporate clients who have their own LLMs trained on their internal data sets, which might provide you with more insight into their practices and relevant information.

## Agents

Another area of LLMs are agents where a LLM is given instructions and then determines tasks to perform, decomposing those tasks into additional tasks., and then performing those tasks. Tools like these and others may be used to take on complex tasks and generate useful results with extraordinarily little human interaction.

This technology is here today, and its use will continue to grow.

## Lawyer generated tools for clients

There will also be opportunities to create simple, easy to use tools for clients or prospective clients. Some lawyers will hone their prompt lawyering skills to generate software-as-service products.

## Removal of limitations

Better models will be created, including models which are more efficient, faster, require less training, and are otherwise superior. Models will have larger context windows. Imagine a context window big enough to include all of the data you have been exposed to in your career.

## *Integration with other technologies*

There will continue to be more and better integration with other technologies including audio, video, and other software applications. The workflows one will be able to create and automate will continue to expand and grow.

## **Conclusions**

Most of these bold statements are not really the future, but actually the present. My sincere hope is that you do not delay in embracing the technology, but learn it, adopt it, and evolve your practice to take advantage of the opportunities for efficiency, process improvement, and enhanced service delivery to your clients.

# ABOUT THE AUTHOR

John D. Goodhue is a patent attorney at Goodhue, Coleman & Owens, P.C. in Des Moines, Iowa, USA. John has always had great passion and curiosity for new technologies. Growing up on a farm in rural Iowa, John received first-hand experience with machinery and technologies and marvels at the evolution of agricultural technologies. John received a degree in computer engineering from Rose-Hulman Institute of Technology (Terre Haute, Indiana) and attended graduate school at Iowa State University (Ames, Iowa). He received his law degree from Drake University (Des Moines, Iowa). Along the way, he was a principal in two different start-ups, and worked for a software company, amongst other experiences. John's primary area of focus is representing clients before the U.S. Patent and Trademark Office in inventions relating to electronics and software technologies including in the agritech, fintech, and artificial intelligence fields. John also works with clients to avoid infringing the rights of others and to assist in patent portfolio valuation and analysis.

www.ingramcontent.com/pod-product-compliance
Lightning Source LLC
Chambersburg PA
CBHW070637220526
45466CB00001B/205